TEAM UP!

Compact and effective activities for building, strengthening and stretching working relationships!

Created by Janis Allen

Quantity discounts are available from the publisher:
BAUDVILLE, INC.
5380 52nd Street SE
Grand Rapids, MI 49512
1-800-728-0888
www.baudville.com

Welcome!

Team   45

Welcome!

Acknowledgements

Debra Sikanas, listening to her customers, conceived this book and made it happen. She offered me valuable suggestions, insightful questions, and good catches in the manner of an equal partner.

If you ever want to see what "respect for a colleague" looks like, just camp out and watch her for a few days. You won't find a better example of respectful teamwork anywhere.

Joe Naimo, Creative Director, brought bright, fresh energy to the printed page. I'm proud to have my plain words brought to such appealing life with Joe's elegant, fun artistry.

Foreword

At Baudville, our aim in creating books is to provide you with material that is informative, fun, and immediately useful to you, the recognition practitioner. From employee induction through teambuilding exercises to retirement celebration ideas, this book will help you to recognize both the contributions and potential of your organization's most valuable resource – people.

This book would not exist without the creative drive of Janis Allen. An outstanding recognition practitioner and teacher for over 25 years, Janis deserves special recognition for her ability to craft books. This involves more than writing; Janis took a concept, sought ideas from Baudville customers, and formatted their ideas for your easy reference and use.

Thanks and kudos are also due to our wonderful customers. You gave freely of your ideas; we simply compiled them and are making them accessible to others. As always, you make our Baudville team grateful. We hope this book inspires you to develop new and fresh activities that you'll share with us – in anticipation of our next *Team Up!* book.

Enjoy,

Debra Sikanas, President
Baudville, Inc.
debras@baudville.com

To Our Readers

At least 61 people have field-tested and refined their ideas to create this book.

All the names you see on the pages are people who are working to make their workplaces more positive, more appreciative of associates, and develop better teamwork and excellent customer service.

These aren't theories. They're the tried-and-true results of creative imaginations and the willingness to try new things – a bit of a professional risk in some cases, as is true of all innovation. These ideas come from brave souls.

We benefit from this broad array of trial and error experiences; you can be sure none of us included activities that didn't work!

You're holding a book that includes two types of activities:

1. Activities used by managers and supervisors to increase recognition, teamwork, or improve customer service within their departments.

2. Activities used by trainers in the classroom to engage participants in effective and fun learning experiences.

Some of these are one-time activities. Some create an ongoing program, which eventually stops being a program and becomes the way you operate as a natural work group.

We have alternated the use of "she" and "he," rather than write clumsily ("He or she should write his or her note and give it to his or her associate when he or she meets his or her goals.").

Contributors who have allowed us to print e-mail addresses have done so because they will be happy to receive questions (or kudos if you like their ideas).

In 25 years as a recognition trainer and consultant, I have, year after year, increased my percentage of classroom time used for activities rather than lecture. At this writing, my training classes average one activity every 18 minutes.

I've found there is no substitute for the active involvement of these experienced and wise participants.

They learn much more and are motivated to do much more outside the classroom... when they TEAM UP! to build, strengthen, and stretch.

Janis Allen
May 1, 2003

Debra Sikanas
May 1, 2003

Recognition

CHAPTER 1

Movie Stars

Goal: Learn recognition practices from the book *Priceless Motivation.*

Number of people: 4 to 30.

Time: 10 minutes to explain; 20 minutes to prepare (in pairs); 5 minutes as part of your department meetings for 17 weekly meetings.

Props: Priceless Motivation, one copy per person (item 92319); flamboyant hats, masks, or costumes; tools of the trade, such as toy telephones, headset, computer, hammer, etc.; bouquets of flowers.

Step-by-step:

1. Distribute copies of *Priceless Motivation.*
2. Group participants in pairs.
3. Turn to the table of contents and explain that you want the pairs to take turns teaching the chapters to the rest of the group.
4. Write numbers 1-17 (for the 17 chapters) on erasable board or flip chart. Determine the number of chapters to assign at the first meeting based on one chapter for every two people in your group. For example, if you have 10 people, draw a line below number 5.
5. Ask pairs to choose which chapter they want to teach, then walk up to the board and put their name next to the number of the chapter. First come, first served! (You'll revisit the list later, when the first five chapters have been taught, and sign up for another chapter, until all 17 are complete.)
6. Ask pairs to prepare a two-act skit demonstrating:

    Act One (Bloopers): The wrong way to practice the chapter's key points

    Act Two (Success at Last): The right way to practice the key points
7. The skits will be performed at the beginning of your weekly department meetings, and will last a maximum of 2 minutes each.
8. Lay out costumes, masks, hats, and other toy "tools of the trade" (such as phones, headsets, hammers, etc.) and invite the pairs to select their costumes and props.
9. Take pictures during performances and post on department bulletin board.
10. Bring bouquets of flowers to give actors as they take their bows.
11. See next page for an Academy Awards activity to follow this one!

Academy Awards

Goal: Celebrate the Movie Stars activity from the previous page.

Number of people: 4 to 30.

Time: One hour.

Props: Red carpet; boom box with music (CD or tape); clip-on black bow ties and large fake diamond necklaces and earrings; and awards for participants: Shining Star desk awards (item 73928), Shining Star Squeezable Praise™ (92572), Star beanbags (93085), or You are a Star desk toy (73945).

Step-by-step:

1. When pairs have performed all 17 chapters of *Priceless Motivation,* celebrate by having a Red Carpet day, when everyone is invited to dress in "Academy Award attire." Walk the red carpet (complete with interviewers and paparazzi) in a conference room or down a hall, or into the front door, if you're brave!

2. Ask each person who acted parts in the skits to come to the front of the room. Give Shining Star desk awards or Shining Star Squeezable Praise to all.

3. Ask for speeches.

4. Turn on music to cut off speeches that get too long – just for the fun of it!

5. Enjoy a catered ceremony lunch, then call your agents!

This idea created by: Janis Allen • janisallen@yahoo.com • www.janisallen.com

Recognition Board Roundup

Goal: Reinforce and therefore increase the use of recognition within your team. Increase team behaviors that help achieve the team goal or vision.

Number of people: 4 to 20.

Time: 5 minutes each week as an agenda item at your team meeting.

Props: Events Stickers (item 73696) or F.I.S.H. Stickers (75410); Recognition Board (73673) or F.I.S.H. Board (75405).

Step-by-step:

1. Assign a symbol from the Events Stickers or F.I.S.H. Stickers to each team member, and give each person a supply of his sticker symbol.

2. Each week, select one team behavior that you want to recognize and post it on the Recognition or F.I.S.H. board. This will change from week to week. One week, it might be "completing customer requests in one call." The next week, it might be "assisting a teammate."

3. At your weekly team meeting, announce the team behavior of the week and write it at the top of the board as a title.

4. Ask that team members post on the Recognition Board the names of people they "caught" doing that week's behavior, a short description of the behavior, and place their sticker symbol beside it. Example: "John helped me format my spreadsheet so that the sales figures were easier to understand." Put your sticker on the board beside your comment.

5. The goal for each person is to use 3-5 stickers each week.

6. Set a team goal for each week on the cumulative number of stickers given by all. Plan a small team celebration when the goal is reached. Example: for a team of 6, set a goal for 18 stickers to be posted that week. If the goal is met, celebrate with an extra 15 minutes for lunch.

7. Review your results each week at your team meeting and celebrate achieving your goal with the reward you had planned.

Pop Go the Balloons

Goal: Co-worker recognition.

Number of people: 4 to 12.

Time: 15 minutes.

Props: Balloons in assorted colors,
T.E.A.M. Post-It® note cube (item 93337);
F.I.S.H. pen (93339); You Are a Star pen (93338).

Step-by-step:

1. Ask each person to think of two positive actions he has noticed over the last two weeks, one in each of two different co-workers. Then write separate recognition notes to those co-workers describing their behaviors. Participants should begin each note with the name of the person whose behavior is being described, and sign their names.

2. Instruct each participant to select two balloons of the same color, roll up the notes, and insert them into balloons. Inflate and tie the balloons.

3. Toss the balloons into the center of the room.

4. When everyone is finished, each person picks up a balloon of a different color than the ones they inflated.

5. One by one, each person pops the balloon by sitting on it, then retrieves the note, and reads it aloud. He then presents the note to the person who about whom it was written.

6. Repeat until all balloons have been popped and notes read.

7. Proud owners are invited to post their notes inside or outside their work areas (on a cubicle nameplate, for example), but this is voluntary.

This idea created by: Janis Allen • janisallen@yahoo.com • www.janisallen.com

Give Yourselves a Hand

Goal: Celebrate the use of recognition by team members.
Number of people: 5 to 16.
Time: 5 minutes or less as an agenda item at weekly team meetings.
Props: "52 Ways to Deal Recognition" deck of cards (item 73967).

Step-by-step:

1. Pass around the "52 Ways" deck of cards to team members at your weekly team meeting.
2. Ask each team member to pick a card with a recognition activity that they want to try that week and keep the card a secret.
3. Ask each person to perform their chosen activity (whatever their card suggests) that week without letting their team members know what they have chosen.
4. At the next team meeting, ask each member to "show their card" to reveal what recognition activity they performed.
5. For each activity performed, put that person's card in the center of the table.
6. Set goals and rewards in proportion to the number of people in your group. For example, for 3 performed, you might offer everyone on the team 10 minutes off early. For 4 performed, 15 minutes off early. When everyone on the team reports that they performed their activity, order pizza for lunch that day.
7. To keep this activity fresh ask team members to brainstorm a list of different rewards each month.

You've Got Mail

Goal: Let individuals know how their co-workers value them.

Number of people: 4 to 16.

Time: 20-45 minutes, depending on the number in the group.

Props: T.E.A.M. border paper (item 22048), T.E.A.M. reward seals (61267), T.E.A.M. stamped certificate folders (32194BL).

Step-by-step:

1. One week before the meeting, the leader of a group sends a series of e-mails to everyone in the group, asking them to reply by stating one valuable behavior they've observed in a particular co-worker. For example, the first e-mail asks, "Please reply by naming one behavior you value about Shawn Jones." The second, separate e-mail asks, "Please reply by naming one behavior you value about Joe Turner," and so on. Send separate e-mails naming each team member so that you won't need to separate multiple comments within a single e-mail.

2. Print each e-mail response on T.E.A.M. border paper, affix a T.E.A.M. seal and your initials or a short positive comment next to the seal.

3. Put all notes for each individual into a T.E.A.M. certificate folder, and present the folders full of e-mails to each person in a meeting.

4. Allow time for all team members to open and read their mail.

5. On a voluntary basis, each person is invited to read one comment aloud.

6. The leader then asks the group:
   a. "How do you feel?"
   b. "Do these notes make you want to do anything in particular?"
   c. "When do you want to do this again?"

This idea created by: Lynnette Younggren • team@voyager.net

Island of Stars

Goal: Vote your co-workers "onto the Island" by recognizing their achievements with a Pocket Praise® card.

Number of people: Unlimited.

Time: 45 seconds per person recognized, plus 5 - 7 minutes at team meetings.

Props: You Are a Star co-worker recognition system (item 93555); You Are a Star receipt cards (93561); large plate or bowl; sand; construction paper; and crayons.

Step-by-step:

1. Draw and color two or three palm trees on construction paper. Cut them out and fold them vertically or cut them out two at a time and tape the tops together so that they'll stand up on "the island."

2. Mound clean sand (available at building supply stores, and sometimes at toy stores for children's sand boxes) on the plate or bowl. Place your construction paper palm trees on it. Make a small sign that says "Star Island." Tape the sign to the plate or bowl. Place this in the team meeting room or other central location. If in doubt, ask your team where to place it so that it will be seen daily.

3. Announce to your team that we are creating "Star Island" to recognize the good and helpful things that people do each week. Examples: help a co-worker, create a new project that helps the team mission, help a customer, stay late to complete a project or work order, etc.

4. Show team members the You Are a Star Co-worker Recognition System holder and note cards and explain that they can fill out a card whenever they notice anyone performing a helpful behavior. They are to give that person the part that says "Award Receipt," and tell them that you appreciate what they just did. Take the part that says "You Are a Star," fill out the person's name and what they did, fold it into a "tent," and place it on the dish representing "Star Island." You've just voted them onto the island. (Nobody gets voted off.)

5. At team meetings, ask each person to announce who they "voted onto the island" and why. Lead the team in applauding each person as their behavior is named.

6. Variation: At the end of a month or six weeks, hold a "luau" barbeque lunch for all who were voted onto the island during that time period. Ask each person to take their card(s) from "Star Island" and tape them up at their work stations or tool boxes. Begin the process of voting people onto the island again.

Open House for Employee Recognition and Retention

Goal: Make it easy for leaders to recognize and retain valued associates.

Number of people: Unlimited.

Time: 8 hours to prepare; one hour per quarter for leaders participating.

Props: Trivia quiz or fun exercise leaders can use with their staff; poster paper with write-ups of department recognition stories; recognition resources: books and educational materials; post cards and Pocket Praise® cards, candy, pens and notepads, certificates; flip chart and markers; shopping bags; clip boards with "price lists" of recognition items; refreshments.

Step-by-step:

1. Once per quarter, set up a "Pat on the Back" room to display write-ups of ideas used by your departments in a wall display that will make it easy for participants to walk around the room and get new recognition ideas.
2. Set up a flip chart near the end of this display.
3. Set up a Recognition Store where they may "buy" recognition props/gifts.
4. Invite all members of your leadership group, and welcome them with a trivia quiz or something fun they can take back and use with their staff.
5. When participants arrive, give each of them:
    a. Notepad to record ideas they get during their tour of the room
    b. Copy of the newsletter "Pat on the Back"
6. On the flip chart, ask them to jot down (vary this from quarter to quarter):
    a. The ideas they plan to use during the next three months
    b. The last person they recognized: who, what, how, and when
7. When they arrive at the Recognition Store, give each person a bag and a clipboard with a price list (ask them to circle items they wish to "buy").
8. Last, invite them to the food table for refreshments and idea-sharing. Display books on recognition, teamwork, motivation, and leadership.
9. One month later, send an e-mail to all participants summarizing the ideas presented to keep everyone motivated until next quarter's event.
10. Place all ideas on your company's intranet for future reference.
11. Now, get lots of help to "strike the set" and take tomorrow off! Whew!

This idea created by: Sue Ferguson • sferguson@grhs.net
Great River Medical Center, West Burlington, IA

Patient Satisfaction Gets Positive Recognition

Goal: Give special recognition to medical professionals who make improvements in patient satisfaction survey results.

Number of people: Unlimited.

Time: 3 hours for preparation; 20 minutes to present.

Props: T.E.A.M. border paper (item 21080BL), T.E.A.M. Raising the Standard lapel pins (62881).

Step-by-step:

1. When you have patient satisfaction survey results for departments, print the data on border paper for correspondence and meetings with the departments.

2. Selecting areas that offer opportunities for improvement, ask each group to set goals for "raising their standard" before the next survey.

3. At the end of the period (six months, for example), present certificates to department managers or to each individual who reached their goal.

4. Additionally, present matching T.E.A.M. Raising the Standard lapel pins to each team for this important achievement in patient care.

Healthcare Honors Volunteers and Professionals

Goal: Recognize volunteers and professionals and get to know each other.
Number of people: Unlimited.
Time: 90 minutes
Props: You Make the Difference border paper (item 23276), You Make the Difference certificates (23532); balloons, colored napkins, paper plates, cups, and utensils.

Step-by-step:

1a. Write appreciation letters to hospice volunteers and healthcare professionals. Print them on You Make the Difference border paper, and mail to their homes or offices.

   OR

1b. Plan appreciation coffee or luncheon for both volunteers and healthcare professionals.

2. Decorate your room in the colors of your organization. Use balloons, colored napkins, paper plates, utensils, and cups to add to the color and festive look.

3. After the meal or refreshments, ask each person in turn to introduce herself and tell where she was born, and how long she's been in healthcare.

4. Print certificates of appreciation for both volunteers and healthcare professionals (doctors, radiologists, social workers, nurses, and others) who assist patients and their families.

5. Present the certificates, then invite all to tell stories about positive patient events they've witnessed; perhaps events others weren't able to see, as a way to share the positive effects of the work of all present.

These ideas created by: Joann Robinson • hospiceofnwil@blkhawk.net • Hospice of Northwest Illinois and Sharon Hesselmeyer •shesselmeyer@wellnesscommunitystl.org • The Wellness Community of Greater St. Louis

F.I.S.H.ing Tackle

Goal: Give supervisors ideas and tools to recognize their associates.

Number of people: Unlimited.

Time: One hour.

Props: Fishing tackle boxes – one per supervisor.

Step-by-step:

1. To spread the F.I.S.H. Philosophy (Play, Be There, Make Their Day, Choose Your Attitude), assemble recognition props for each tackle box. Some props might include certificates, sticky note pads, Pocket Praise® cards, Milestone charms, candies, stickers, etc.

2. Give the boxes to supervisors to use for simple, fun, and timely recognition for their associates' good performances.

3. Catch the big ones!

This idea created by: Mark Lenz • mark.lenz@us.bosch.com • Bosch Sumter, Sumter, SC

Time Off With Pay for Behaviors and Results

Goal: Recognize goal achievement.

Number of people: Unlimited.

Time: 30 minutes per week.

Props: T.E.A.M. tokens (item 73935), Pocket Praise® You Make the Difference pop-up cards (75309).

Step-by-step:

1. Set and communicate your department goals, along with the individual team behaviors that are steps to meeting these goals.

2. As you see team members demonstrating these behaviors, write a short, specific description of their behavior in a Pocket Praise card, insert a T.E.A.M. token, and present them at your regular meeting.

3. Read what you've written to the group so that everyone will be reminded of the behaviors which get recognition and tokens.

4. When the overall department goal is reached, continue to give out recognition tokens in Pocket Praise cards.

5. Each person may redeem each token he has earned for 15 minutes paid time off. This time off can be accumulated and awarded weekly, monthly, or quarterly. The general rule is to award the time off as immediately as people want to use it and when the demands of your business will permit.

6. Suggest that team members attach their tokens inside the pages of their daily planners or put them in a clear container on their desks, to serve as reminders of the rewards of practicing these goal-achieving behaviors every day.

This idea created by: Debbie Holcomb • Debbie_Holcomb@experienceworks.org
Experience Works, Inc., Lincoln, NE

When the Words Won't Come

Goal: Encourage managers to offer personalized, meaningful recognition to individuals.

Number of people: Unlimited.

Time: 15 minutes per individual to write and deliver cards.

Props: You Make the Difference receipt cards (item 75301).

Step-by-step:

1. Some managers have trouble finding the right words to write a formal letter of recognition to deserving staff. To help them, supply them with You Make the Difference receipt cards.

2. Print your company logo inside the card if you wish.

3. Make these available to your managers and encourage them to use the cards.

4. Collect the receipt portions of the cards.

5. Forward these receipts to the managers of those sending praise cards, so that they can "recognize the recognizers." When they do this, recognition will multiply!

Actions Speak Louder Than Words

Goal: Use body language to send a strong recognition message.
Number of people: 2 (you and one other).
Time: 1-5 minutes.
Props: None.

Step-by-step:

1. When an individual gives you a report or project which you know she's worked hard to complete, or she's proud of, make a special effort to use your body language to give her your complete attention.

2. Use as many forms of body language as you can to send the message that you're giving this work your full attention, such as:

    a. When you accept the document, put down anything else you're holding, even a pen.

    b. If you're at your desk or in your office, stand and walk away from other papers, the computer screen, or any distraction while you study the document. If it's a long document, scan only the important parts for now.

    c. Comment about what you value in this work, and then continue to hold the document in both hands while you talk. Yes, both hands.

    d. Point to specific parts of the document which you value.

    e. If you're headed to another office or to a meeting, take it with you. Hold it next to your chest while you walk, or

    f. Clear off a special space on your desk (while the person watches) and lay the document there.

    g. Pick it up again when you're referring to it verbally.

    h. Keep it uncovered by other papers in this prominent space on your desk for a few days.

    i. Using a red pen, write positive comments on the pages where you find something valuable, and show to the creator later.

3. Set a goal: see if you can use at least five of these body language recognition ideas during the coming week.

 This idea created by: Janis Allen • janisallen@yahoo.com • www.janisallen.com

Recognition By Walking Around

Goal: Catch your associates doing something right – early in the day.

Number of people: 2 - 20.

Time: 10 minutes.

Props: None.

Step-by-step:

1. At the beginning of your workday, before checking e-mail, voicemail, or looking at the projects on your desk, take 10 minutes to walk around the areas where your associates work, looking for valuable behaviors to recognize.

2. Tell co-workers that this is your Recognition Tour, and that during these 10 minutes, you're focusing only on what's being done well, not problem-solving or goal-setting.

3. Look for people engaging in positive behaviors, even those that are usually taken for granted, such as:

    a. Starting work promptly

    b. Picking up the phone after one ring

    c. Speaking kindly or professionally to a customer

    d. Offering to assist a co-worker

    e. Demonstrating safe work practices or using safety equipment

    f. Smiling

    g. _____

4. People will naturally stop you to tell you about problems. Set a time to discuss these later. Explain that you want to finish your Recognition Tour, then you'll be available.

5. Do this early in your workday, before the monsters of problems and challenges begin devouring you alive!

Everyday Heroes

Goal: Recognize individuals who have successfully resolved a challenging issue or assignment, or performed an act which exemplifies your mission.

Number of people: Unlimited.

Time: 30 minutes to prepare; present awards during regular meetings.

Props: Pride certificate paper (item 8BGP31), Achievement foil seals (61258), We're Celebrating You! Rich Rewards™ chocolates (92920), Stars and Confetti celebration cellophane bags (93062), Achievement lapel pins (73675), Formal Assortment Pocket Praise® cards (72600).

Step-by-step:

1. Select individuals who have:
   a. Resolved a challenging issue
   b. Completed a difficult assignment
   c. Performed a single act which exemplifies a commitment to your mission
2. Using award paper, create an Everyday Heroes certificate with foil seal.
3. Create a written description of each hero's achievement, suitable for posting.
4. Present the awards at a meeting of co-workers.
5. Take a close-up photo of each of your heroes.
6. Post the pictures and the written descriptions of their heroic acts on an Everyday Heroes bulletin board.
7. As a memento, present each Everyday Hero with a cellophane bag which includes a lapel pin, candy, and a personal Pocket Praise note from someone significant to the person. Optional: put the bag of goodies in a keepsake coffee mug.
8. Take individual pictures of each of the newest heroes in front of the Everyday Heroes board, holding their certificate.
9. Mail this picture to the individual, accompanied by a letter from a member of top management.
10. When the bulletin board is completed, ask all your heroes to assemble and pose for a group photo in front of the board. Then mail copies of the group photos to their homes with a personal congratulatory note.

This idea created by: Anna Frankel • afrankel@dutchess-arc.org
NYSARC, Inc., Dutchess County Chapter, Poughkeepsie, NY (New York State Assoc. for Retarded Citizens)

Summer School's Cool!

Goal: Make summer school teachers and students feel special.

Number of people: Unlimited.

Time: One hour per week.

Props: T.E.A.M. Clipart (item 12853), I.D. Maker Express (item 13924), lollipops, Pocket Praise® Pop-ups (72601).

Step-by-step:

1. Make name badges for summer employees to help everyone get to know them quickly and make them feel part of your team.
2. Using T.E.A.M. Clipart, create certificates for summer school staff and student recognition. For example:
   a. Custodians who are rarely recognized
   b. Migrant Student of the Year
   c. _____
3. Use Pocket Praise cards to send a colorful keepsake to people who:
   a. Send you information during the day
   b. Take the initiative to solve problems
   c. Go the extra mile to help a student succeed
   d. Take extra time to communicate with co-workers
   e. Contact parents for support or to give good news
   f. _____ (your choice)
4. Tape lollipops to the Pocket Praise cards
5. At summer school graduation, present certificates to students who are receiving academic achievement awards.

Razzle Dazzle Reception

Goal: Create a special recognition reception for a large healthcare group.
Number of people: 200-400.
Time: 2 to 3 weeks to prepare, 1 to 1½ hours for the event.
Props: Presentation FUNdamentals, (item 13983); gifts for honorees, such as: You Are a Star baskets (92909), You Make the Difference gift mugs (93976), Pocket Praise® Mini Awards (73644), Desktop Gallery Awards (32782), 52 Ways to Deal Recognition cards (73967), *Priceless Motivation* (92319); *The Joy of Recognition* (92737), Extraordinary poster assortment (73996),; Framed Praise (33120SV), Recognition Board (73673), You Make a Difference gift set (94054), You Are a Star gift set (92909), You Make the Difference travel tumblers (95150), Applause clappers (93506GD), Shining Star Squeezable Praise™ (92572), and Celebration Star celebration tumblers (92463).

Step-by-step:

1. Give higher-level recognition – including mementos – to associates who have received private or low-key recognition at department or individual levels, by creating a quarterly Recognition Reception to let their co-workers and top managers know of their achievements.

2. Invite these associates and top managers to a catered reception, where a senior member of management gives a brief keynote of welcome and congratulations.

3. Create a Wall of Fame to showcase the honorees.

4. Create a slide show using Presentation FUNdamentals to introduce recognition programs and efforts, and showcase each department's best practices.

5. Ask each recipient to come forward. The senior leader hands her a memento (from selection of props above) and shakes her hand.

6. Categories for recognition (may vary by quarter) are:
   a. "You're Super": individuals who have been given recognition by staff, patients, family members, or visitors
   b. "Shining Star": individuals who achieved their goals in service competency, teamwork, performance, and respect for individuals
   c. Employee Suggestion winners
   d. Department-based performance award recipients

7. Take plenty of photos for your newsletter, website, and bulletin boards.

8. Eat and enjoy!

This idea created by: Denise White • dwhite@med.umich.edu • University of Michigan Health System

M & M's

Goal: Recognize customer service associates who go the extra mile for customers.

Number of people: Unlimited.

Time: 1 minute per person.

Props: Applause, Applause Rich Rewards™ chocolates (item 92674), M & M's, or any favorite candy.

Step-by-step:

1. Notice when a customer service associate:
   a. Exceeds your expectations for the customer
   b. Offers extra assistance
   c. Helps a co-worker
   d. Stays late to complete a customer request
   e. Remains calm and professional with an irate customer
   f. _____

2. Tell the person immediately what you've noticed and give her the candy.

This idea created by: Debra Williamson • dwilli1022@aol.com • Operations Specialist, Sacramento, CA

Cheers for Peers

Goal: Encourage individuals to recognize each other by giving them fun and easy tools.

Number of people: Unlimited.

Time: 3 minutes per person giving recognition.

Props: Bulletin board in each department, Fun Assortment Pocket Praise® cards (item 72466).

Step-by-step:

1. Introduce "Cheers for Peers" to everyone in your company. Explain that it's an opportunity for everyone – no matter what their job or level in the organization – to recognize others for:

   a. Specific performance results or efforts
   b. Giving assistance
   c. Achieving project milestones
   d. Achieving length-of-service milestones
   e. Great service to a customer
   f. _____

2. Give supplies of Pocket Praise cards to all and ask them to write notes which they will:

   a. Post on the "Cheers for Peers" board
   b. Send a copy to the HR department

3. Make photos of your bulletin board with its praise cards, then remove and give the cards to their "honorees."

4. Keep the board "fresh" by making room for new praise cards, which keeps people stopping by to see what's new.

Spinning for Recognition

Goal: Boost morale and increase peer recognition.

Number of people: Unlimited.

Time: 1 minute per person giving recognition.

Props: Large round board designed to spin, mounted on bulletin board; slips of paper showing employees' names; two huge thank-you cards mounted on bulletin board.

Step-by-step:

1. Construct a large wheel which can spin and has a stopper/pointer.
2. Construct it with a surface on which you can attach small slips of paper, each with an employee's name printed on it.
3. Mount it on a bulletin board in a common area.
4. Select 10-15 employees each week whose names will be placed on the wheel, based on recommendations by their supervisors or co-workers, and attach the names.
5. Mount two huge home-made thank-you cards on the bulletin board on either side of the wheel.
6. On a pre-announced schedule, invite employees to gather at the wheel, and select someone to spin the wheel.
7. When it stops, ask the spinner to call out the name positioned at the pointer.
8. Invite all employees to write a note to that person on the card at left of the wheel, noting something about that person's performance that is valuable.
9. Repeat with a different person as spinner, and invite the group to write notes to the second person whose name is at the "stop," on the large card which is at the right of the wheel.
10. At next week's "spinning," give the large cards to the honorees. Then mount new blank cards on the board and do it all again to keep that wheel turning and peer recognition moving!

52 Ways to Deal Magic

Goal: Make it easy for sales managers to give recognition.
Number of people: Unlimited.
Time: 10 seconds per person recognized.
Props: "52 Ways to Deal Recognition" deck of cards (item 73967).

Step-by-step:

1. To develop the theme, "The Magic of Recognition and Reward," invite your sales managers to draw a card from your "52 Ways" deck.

2. Challenge them to implement the idea which is presented on the card they draw (some cards have insights or quotes; here they can be creative and expand those ideas to implementation actions, or if no action comes to mind, let them draw again).

3. Let the managers know that their actions will "Make Magic."

4. An example: if a manager draws the card suggesting "make recognition easy by providing recognition forms at high-traffic areas like the copy machine or employee lounge," this would be a high-visibility project which "Makes Magic."

5. When managers report that they've implemented the idea from their card, pull a rabbit out of a hat and treat them to lunch!

This idea created by: Kathy Gilkey • k.gilkey@kleinet.com • Klein Financial, Inc., MN

Helpful High 5

Goal: Recognize and increase the frequency of associates helping each other.
Number of people: Unlimited.
Time: 10 seconds per person recognized.
Props: High 5 buttons (item 73882).

Step-by-step:

1. When an associate goes beyond the call of duty to help one of his associates, the associate recognizing the behavior gives him a High 5 button.
2. The buttons are presented at department meetings or social gatherings.
3. Recipients are asked to wear their buttons for the entire day, and then to display them in their cubicles or offices.

This idea created by: Sharyn Rahl • Sharyn_Rahl@dart.biz • Dart Container Corp., Mason, MI

25

Strike Gold

Goal: Give immediate recognition which can be turned into loot!
Number of people: Unlimited.
Time: 1 minute.
Props: You Make the Difference Cheerful Change™ coins (item 74009).

Step-by-step:

1. Ask associates to look for behaviors among their co-workers which are above and beyond their job duties, and nominate them to receive recognition.

2. Give a coin to the person whose nomination is accepted, and tell her what her co-worker has noticed and nominated her for doing.

3. When an associate accumulates 10 coins, he may redeem them for a full day off with pay.

4. Can't wait? After an associate receives two or more coins, he can redeem each one for a $5.00 value gift certificate from:
    a. Merchants
    b. Restaurants
    c. Movie theatres
    d. _____

5. Form an ARM Committee (Awards, Recognition, and Motivation) to keep up with recognition given and its value, for tracking expenditures. This information can also be used to assist your managers in choosing individuals for further recognition, and used as a factor in promotion decisions.

This idea created by: Roberta M. Miller • RMiller@BankofLenawee.com • Bank of Lenawee, Adrian, MI

Muffin Monday

Goal: Reward your team for performance, and start the week off warmly!
Number of people: Only limited by your oven size.
Time: 1 hour.
Props: Homemade muffins, coffee, tea, and juice.

Step-by-step:

1. Set and announce weekly performance goals in:
   a. Production
   b. Quality
   c. Customer service
   d. _____
2. When your team meets their weekly goal, announce on Friday that you're bringing muffins in on Monday to show your appreciation.
3. Eat, drink, and be productive, anticipating the next Muffin Monday!

Treasure Hunt for Specificity

Goal: Learn how to give meaningful recognition to an individual.
Number of people: 2-20.
Time: 15 minutes.
Props: Copies of letter (see Appendix, page 111) one per person; answer key (see Appendix, page 113).

Step-by-step:

1. Give copies of the sample recognition letter to each person in your group.
2. Explain that this letter is a treasure trove of specific elements which made it effective (meaningful and motivating to the receiver).
3. Tell them that Roger is president of a publishing company and Bernadette is an editor.
4. Ask the group to read the letter silently and go on a treasure hunt for every word which contributes to its effectiveness. Ask them to circle every one they find, and turn their sheets over when finished. Allow five minutes.
5. Ask people to tell you what words they've circled and why. Tally the number found. Add any new ones you've found that they've missed.
6. Make the point that specificity is the key to meaningfulness.
7. A little secret: Bernadette joked that for the rest of her career, she'll never write a headline without including "stunned" and murky."

To: Bernadette Casey
From: J. Roger Friedman
Subject: Headlines

Dear Bernadette:
I've been impressed with the headlines in the last few issues of Drug Store News. They read well and gave a sense of urgency. The November 18th issue is an example of what I am referring to – I liked the headlines on page 1 and on page 3. The words "stunned" and "murky" are excellent choices of words. Congratulations.

Sincerely,

Roger

J. Roger Friedman

Cc: Fred Filer, Marie Griffin, Bruce Matzner, Sandy Sutton*

This idea created by: Janis Allen • janisallen@yahoo.com • www.janisallen.com

Auction

Goal: Increase co-worker recognition and have some fun.
Number of people: Unlimited.
Time: 20 minutes per auction.
Props: You Made My Day team tokens (item 75217), gavel.

Step-by-step:

1. Empower employees to give tokens to each other for "good deeds" such as:
   a. Valuable team actions
   b. Good catches to prevent problems
   c. Training a newcomer
   d. Taking a message
   e. Getting someone "unstuck" from a software problem
   f. _____

2. Once a month, hold an auction where employees can bid on fun items, using their tokens to pay. Auction off items like:
   a. Extra day of vacation
   b. Massage
   c. Manicure
   d. Gift certificates
   e. Lunch with supervisor at favorite restaurant
   f. _____

3. Ask senior managers to take turns being the auctioneer, complete with gavel and fast talk!

4. Employees will always be LOOKING for ways to recognize co-workers if a fun event like this one awaits.

5. Sold… to the highest bidder!

This idea created by: Debbie Strever • DStrever@Billingsfcu.org • Billings Federal Credit Union, Billings, MT

Ziploc Your Recognition

Goal: Make it easy for your colleagues to give recognition – anytime!

Number of people: Unlimited.

Time: 10 minutes per manager.

Props: Ziploc® baggies, Fun Assortment Pocket Praise® cards (item 72466), list of recommended behaviors to recognize.

Step-by-step:

1. Prepare baggies filled with:
    a. An assortment of Pocket Praise cards
    b. Lists of behaviors to recognize
2. At a meeting, announce yourself as "The Bag Lady" (this will be even funnier if you happen to be a man), perhaps even dressing the part. Distribute filled baggies to managers and supervisors.
3. Ask them to unzip their baggies, and to be generous writing Pocket Praise notes to employees for all kinds of things (i.e. "Thanks for volunteering to help Sue with her tough assignment," or "I appreciate the way you handled that angry client on the phone," etc.).
4. Make a place on your bulletin board titled "Pocket Praise Comes Out of the Pocket" and encourage recipients of cards to post them if they're willing.

This idea created by: Kris Taranec • ktaranec@hospicehavasu.org
Hospice of Havasu, Lake Havasu City, Arizona

Love Those Volunteers

Goal: Make city or county volunteers feel appreciated.

Number of people: Unlimited.

Time: 15 minutes per volunteer recognized.

Props: Black Tie gold foil certificates (item 22904WT), Volunteer certificate seals (62230), black satin award ribbons (61253), Volunteers Make the Difference buttons (73885), Stars gold foil mini-seals (63461), lunch.

Step-by-step:

1. If your city or county organization is blessed with volunteers who donate their time, talents, and energy, send them a keepsake to show you don't take them for granted and that you value their work.

2. Dress up your awards by printing each volunteer's name and volunteer activity on a Black Tie foil certificate, and ask your organization's president or chief executive to sign it. Attach black satin award ribbon with a gold seal, either your organization's seal or a purchased one.

3. Option: Hold an appreciation luncheon to recognize volunteers. When they arrive, give them a Volunteers Make the Difference button.

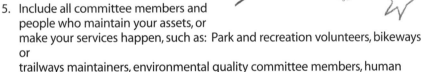

4. For new volunteers or first-time attendees, place a gold foil mini-seal on their buttons, to cue your veteran volunteers to make them feel welcome.

5. Include all committee members and people who maintain your assets, or make your services happen, such as: Park and recreation volunteers, bikeways or trailways maintainers, environmental quality committee members, human rights committee members, economic development board members, planning commission members, public safety volunteers, telecommunications and technology volunteers, festival planning groups, etc.

6. Remember people who sit on boards, not just those who do physical work!

These ideas created by: Tammy Schutta • TCHUTTA@CI.SHOREVIEW.MN.US • City of Shoreview, Shoreview, MN Penny Peterson • Peterson@dancris.com • General Federation of Women's Clubs, Phoenix, AZ

Fancy Titles Recognition

Goal: Do some fun nicknaming with your personalized recognition.
Number of people: Unlimited.
Time: 1 hour per person recognized.
Props: Hand-decorated mugs.

Step-by-step:

1. Create recognition gifts for co-workers at a "paint your own ceramics" shop.
2. Personalize each mug with a fun depiction of a skill each person has.
3. Paint your colleagues' names on one side of each mug.
4. On the other side, paint your fancy title for each, highlighting a favorite characteristic:
   a. Maddy… Queen of Trashing Targets
   b. Michael… Chief Collaborator of Creativity
   c. Meredith… Maven of Marketing Mayhem
   d. Debra… Empress of Exceptional Editing
   e. Joe… Admiral of Awesome Artistry
   f. _____
5. Guaranteed smiles.

This idea created by: Glain Roberts-McCabe • groberts@micaworld.com
MICA Seminars, Toronto, ON, Canada

F.I.S.H. - Fresh Ideas Start Here

Goal: Involve all associates in a fun idea-generating ongoing project.
Number of people: Unlimited.
Time: 1 hour per week.
Props: Goldfish™ crackers, F.I.S.H. candy (item 95087); Think Outside the Bowl F.I.S.H. poster (73980); Fresh Ideas Start Here suggestion system (93380); F.I.S.H. Squeezable Praise™ (93258); F.I.S.H. border paper (23118); F.I.S.H. key chains (93134); F.I.S.H. mouse pads (93459); Fish stickers (available at Party City and other stores); Fish cards for accumulating stickers (designed and printed by you).

Step-by-step:

1. Introduce the F.I.S.H. concepts to your organization, emphasizing: Play!, Make their day!, Be there! and Choose your attitude!

2. Using the F.I.S.H. suggestion system, invite everyone to submit fresh ideas for improving your business.

3. Invite everyone to nominate co-workers for a "fish," for going beyond the call of duty.

4. Award fish stickers to those nominated. When an associate accumulates 20 stickers on his fish card, he may redeem them for $20.00.

5. At month's end, publish a Fishing Report on F.I.S.H. border paper of all ideas, along with the creators' names. Send to all associates, and post it on a bulletin board beside F.I.S.H. poster.

6. At a monthly Fishing Trip meeting, reward the idea creators with their choice of F.I.S.H. items. Give out crackers and candy.

7. Set a challenging but achievable goal for the number of fish stickers to earn annually. Offer each person who achieves the goal $100.00.

8. Hold an annual Fishing Trip, when everyone is invited to dress for going fishing, and present the monetary awards. Invite associates to share one of the F.I.S.H. ideas they've implemented during the year.

These ideas created by: April Girard • agirard@landata.com • Landata Information Services, Houston, TX

CARE

Goal: Make it easy for managers to give recognition.
Number of people: Unlimited.
Time: 1 hour per month.
Props: Kraft Paper gift bags (item 92433); Shooting Star key rings (95159); Making the Difference pens (73965); Shining Star milestone charms (75213); Applause, Applause Rich Rewards™ chocolates (92674).

Step-by-step:

1. Create a CARE team of representatives from different departments or sites. CARE means Creative Activities Recognizing Employees.

2. Managers are much more likely to give recognition if they have the supplies, so ask the CARE team to create CARE packages for distributing to all managers and supervisors at their monthly meetings (a new package each month).

3. Each month's package has a theme, for example:
   a. A holiday in that month
   b. A special project the organization is involved in
   c. _____

4. Included in the CARE packages are:
   a. Articles or information about the importance of recognizing employees
   b. A template or sample of what to write in a thank-you card
   c. Key chains or pens
   d. Shining Star charms
   e. Logo pins
   f. Rich Rewards chocolate coins
   g. _____

5. Give each manager a 3-ring binder for filing her articles and information received in each month's CARE package, complete with a colorful "CARE" cover page.

This idea created by: Anita Allen • anitaallen@chiwest.com • Linus Oakes Retirement Center, Roseburg, OR

Spin the Bottle

Goal: Share appreciation among team members in a fun way.
Number of people: Up to 16.
Time: 15-30 minutes.
Props: A bottle.

Step-by-step:

1. Sit in a circle, in chairs or on the floor.
2. Place a bottle on the floor in the center of the circle.
3. Ask a volunteer to spin the bottle.
4. When the bottle stops, the spinner is asked to say something specific that he appreciates about the person the bottle is pointing to.
5. Next, the person who was just spoken about spins the bottle and says what she appreciates about the next person at the "point."
6. Continue until everyone has been spoken about (it's O.K. if some are spoken about multiple times), or set a time limit and just keep going.
7. When time's up, no one will want to stop!

This idea created by: Elizabeth Peterson • epeterson@oxy.edu • Occidental College, Los Angeles, CA

Keeping Momentum

Goal: Recognize, and support a team that mentors new employees.

Number of people: One per department, plus a coordinator.

Time: 1 hour per week.

Props: You Make the Difference certificate paper (item 23532),
Making the Difference brass lapel pins (73677).

Step-by-step:

1. Form a Momentum Committee for your organization to serve as a driving force to recognize, support, and mentor new employees. Invite one employee per work area, and assign one person as coordinator.

2. Equip this group with training in recognition and mentoring, so that they may serve as leaders in supporting new employees in their respective work areas.

3. At staff meetings, give recognition to these committee members for their work and successes they or others can report in supporting new employees.

4. Present these Momentum Committee members with Making a Difference certificates and pins to help keep that momentum going.

This idea created by: Barb Abeln • Barb.Abeln@state.sd.us • Turtle Creek Youth Program, Redfield, SD

Smiling Volleyball Travels School Halls

Goal: Remind your team to stay focused on its goals.

Number of people: Unlimited.

Time: 15 minutes.

Props: Volleyballs, smiley-face cookies, theme signs, smiley-face t-shirts.

Step-by-step:

1. Establish a theme for your goals for the school year, such as "Don't Worry, Be Happy."

2. Decorate volleyballs with smiley faces (draw with permanent markers).

3. Explain the theme at your back-to-school meeting, and toss all the volleyballs to random members of the group. Ask those who catch them to be on the lookout for colleagues' behaviors which support this year's theme.

4. Brainstorm with the group to generate some examples of behaviors which will support the theme.

5. Ask holders of the volleyballs to pass their smiling volleyballs to colleagues they notice who are exhibiting those behaviors, telling the colleague what they noticed which earned this "traveling trophy." Ask them to write the recipient's name on the ball in permanent marker before passing it on.

6. Give everyone a "Don't Worry, Be Happy" sign and ask them to post in classrooms, restrooms, offices, and lounges.

7. Serve smiley-face-decorated cookies.

8. Ask that whoever has a volleyball bring it to every staff meeting and tell what they did to receive the traveling trophy.

9. At the last staff meeting of the year, give smiley face t-shirts to everyone.

10. Ask that the volleyball traveling trophies be turned in. Have a drawing of every name written on it, and give it as a memento to the winning name drawn.

Praise & Kisses in the School District

Goal: Give recognition to school staff with sweets in the mailboxes.
Number of people: Unlimited.
Time: 3 minutes per person giving recognition.
Props: Hershey's Kisses® candy, WOW Pocket Praise® cards (73161).

Step-by-step:

1. Look around your school, business, or organization for done actions, large or small, which:

    a. Help meet your goals

    b. Help others

2. Write a Pocket Praise note to each person you want to recognize, mentioning the positive action they took.

3. Attach a Kiss.

4. Leave it in her mailbox to find as a surprise, which is a great way to start the day.

This idea created by: Elizabeth Spiro • espiro@sidney.k12.ny.us • Sidney Central School District, Sidney, NY

Making the Difference to Your Customers

Goal: Publicize recognition from customers and co-workers.

Number of people: Unlimited.

Time: One hour per quarter.

Props: You Make the Difference border paper (item 23276); You Make the Difference candles (93969); You Make the Difference trinket box (93285); You Make the Difference key rings (95020); You Make the Difference Post-it® note holder (95191); You Make the Difference Rich Rewards chocolates (93274); You Make the Difference umbrella (95161); You Make the Difference executive portfolio (93916); Making the Difference brass lapel pins (73677); Making the Difference pens (73965); Making the Difference travel tumblers (93971); Making the Difference mouse pads (93972).

Step-by-step:

1. Save all positive comments submitted about employees by customers, and send copies to HR.

2. Recognize in writing (printed on border paper) anyone who meets performance goals or exhibits a customer-oriented positive behavior.

3. At a quarterly "Making a Difference" meeting, give public recognition to every individual who has received these two types of recognition during the quarter. Announce their names and tell about their great behaviors.

4. Invite them to select from whichever items from the above list that you have on hand.

5. Use reminders printed on You Make a Difference border papers to communicate about this program during the year.

Recognition Goes Home

Goal: Let family members know you appreciate their support.

Number of people: One at a time

Time: 10 minutes.

Props: Thank You greeting card assortment (item 75175).

Step-by-step:

1. When one of your employees has spent a lot of extra time on a work project, or worked overtime for several weeks, write a note to his spouse, partner, or even to his children.

2. Express your appreciation for their support and understanding while their spouse, partner, mom, or dad has put valuable time and energy into the project or the work demands. Tell them how much you appreciate the employee, too.

This idea created by: Erin Winkler • Erin.Winkler@VerizonWireless.com • Nashville, TN

The Library Book

Goal: Create a meaningful and lasting tribute.
Number of people: One at a time.
Time: 15 minutes.
Props: A book.

Step-by-step:

1. To give touching recognition to someone who has contributed a singular helpful act, such as a volunteer activity, donate a special book in honor of that person to:

   a. Your organization's library

   b. Your school's library

   c. Your public library (check with them to see if they accept donated books)

2. Place a label in the inside cover stating:

This book is donated in honor of

_____

for

_____

by

_____

_____

Date

3. The honoree will be able to share this with her family and friends for years to come. She'll feel as if they've named a street after her!

Learning Las Vegas-style

Goal: In a fun way, learn the "why's" and "how's" of giving positive recognition.
Number of people: 4 –16 (suggested use: members of one department).
Time: 10 minutes per meeting.
Props: "52 Ways to Deal Recognition" cards (item 73967); green eye shade, sleeve garter, or any "Las Vegas dealer" accessories.

Step-by-step:

1. At a regular meeting, tell your co-workers you'll be dealing poker hands at each meeting to learn "why's" and "how's" of giving recognition.

2. For each meeting, select only one of the four suits of cards, reserving the other three for future meetings.

3. After much elaborate shuffling and cutting of cards, deal one card from that suit to each person face down. Ask them to wait for your instructions before turning over their cards.

   Meeting 1: INSIGHTS suit (HEARTS):

   a. Ask the group: "Why should we give recognition to co-workers?"

   b. Ask them to read their cards. Allow 60 seconds of silence for reading and preparing their answers.

   c. Ask all to answer your question in their own words.

   d. Also, they're permitted to simply read the information from the cards and discuss if they prefer.

   e. Give recognition for all participation.

   Meeting 2: Resources suit (STARS):

   • Deal cards and, giving the group two minutes to prepare, ask them to give mini "book reports" from their cards.

   Meeting 3: Handy Hints suit (HANDS):

   • Deal cards and, giving the group two minutes to prepare, ask them to share a specific way the ideas can be applied here.

   Meeting 4: Tips suit (TEAM GUY):

   • Deal cards and, giving the group two minutes to prepare, ask them to give mini "book reports" from their cards.

This idea created by: Lois Hart, Ed.D. • lhart@seqnet.net
Executive Director, Women's Leadership Institute, Denver CO

Three-way Recognition

Goal: Identify qualities we appreciate in co-workers, employees, and managers.
Number of people: 6-24.
Time: 25 minutes.
Props: Flip chart paper, markers, masking tape, You Make the Difference Pocket Praise® Cards (item 75309), pens.

Step-by-step:

1. Divide participants into three groups: A, B. and C.
2. Ask group A to think about things they appreciate about their co-workers.
3. Ask group B to think about things they appreciate about their managers.
4. Ask group C to think about things they appreciate about their employees.
5. After 10 minutes, ask a spokesperson from each group to share its list.
6. Then ask, "What do you notice about these three lists?"
7. Common responses:
    a. "They're very similar."
    b. "Many of the qualities cut across all three groups."
    c. "I never thought about recognizing 'up' to my manager."
8. Ask the entire group to think about someone they would like to recognize, possibly someone who came to mind while brainstorming.
9. Distribute Pocket Praise cards, and ask each person to write that person a note, identifying:
    a. The quality I appreciate
    b. Why it's important to our organization
10. Ask two or three people, on a volunteer basis, to read their notes to the group.

This idea created by: Theresa Chambers • tcariel@yahoo.com • Ariel Consulting

Team

CHAPTER 2

Essence of Team

Goal: To identify elements of successful teams, and to energize teams.
Number of people: 6-20.
Time: 15 minutes to 1 hour, depending on the number in the group.
Props: Flip chart and markers, You Make the Difference reward seals (item 63265).

Step-by-step:

1. Ask participants to think of a time when they were part of a team which was both successful and rewarding.
2. Draw a vertical line down the length of a flip-chart page. Write "Successful" and "Rewarding" at the top of the two columns and underline them.
3. After each person tells her story, the leader asks the group to name one- or two-word characteristics which made the team successful and/or rewarding. Record these characteristics on your sheet (expect words like "goals," "open communication," "reward at the end," etc.).
4. Ask "What behaviors can we try in the next five days to create this experience for our team?" Record answers on second sheet.
5. Make plans to meet one week later to report behaviors which have been "spotted," and record them on the sheet (from step 4).
6. Ask each person who reports a behavior to place a You Make the Difference seal next to the comment on the paper, and initial.
7. Give recognition to those reporting and doing the behaviors.
8. As a group, schedule another date and time to repeat steps 5-7.
9. Post the flip-chart paper in your work area as an everyday reminder.

This idea created by: Peter Grazier • GOTeams@aol.com • www.teambuildinginc.com

Poster Power

Goal: Recognize individual behaviors which support team values.

Number of people: 2 to 20.

Time: 15 minutes per weekly meeting, then one minute per person per week.

Props: Team Building Posters (ask team to select one from Baudville catalog), Stars mini seals (item 63461), sticky notes.

Step-by-step:

1. Ask team members to select two posters which will become the team's themes for months one and two. Select which one to use first.

2. Display the poster as soon as it arrives.

3. Distribute sticky notes and ask team members to record their own behaviors which support the team value defined by the poster they've selected.

4. Each person is asked to PRINT so that others won't recognize her handwriting. Notes should be posted anonymously right onto the front of the poster.

5. One week later, bring the poster into the meeting room, or gather around the poster as it hangs on the wall. Take turns pulling one note off and reading it aloud, having team members guess who wrote this note.

6. Ask the owner of the note to come clean by saying "Mine!"

7. The owner of each note then signs it and presents it to the manager of the group.

8. The manager keeps all the notes, and over the next 48 hours, adds her note of recognition for this behavior (using back of note if needed), then adds a gold Mini Seal, and personally gives it back to its owner. This provides double-time recognition for behaviors which support team values!

9. While the group is together, ask them to select two more posters so that they can be ordered in time for the next two months' themes, then repeat steps 2-8.

   This idea created by: Janis Allen • janisallen@yahoo.com • www.janisallen.com

ePraise Tips

Goal: Building teamwork.

Number of people: 3 to 20.

Time: 20 minutes

Props: ePraise® software (item 15024), 10 colors of marking pens, T.E.A.M. milestone charms (75212), and milestone cards (75401).

Step-by-step:

1. Go to the ePraise home page and click on Recognition Tips (light bulb icon) at the bottom right. Scroll down to the chart "Key Words and Phrases." Print this table and bring it to a meeting of your team. Enlarge if you have more than eight people.

2. Showing this 42-block chart, ask each team member to select two blocks (first come, first served), that contain a word or phrase that describes the behavior of two of his team members. Team members "claim" blocks by writing the name of a team member in it in colored marker.

3. When everyone's finished, team members take turns stating the behaviors they have observed which prompted them to match the individuals to the squares.

4. Announce that when all 42 squares have at least one name written in them, all team members will receive T.E.A.M. Milestones and Milestone Cards.

5. At the next meeting of this team, repeat steps 2 and 3. It's O.K. to place two or more names in the boxes now.

6. Ask the group's permission to display the chart in your department, and decide where to put it.

Make Change Where You Work

Goal: Start a chain reaction of praise, emphasizing "change for the better."
Number of people: 3-22.
Time: 5 minutes to explain; 30 seconds per person per day.
Props: Cheerful Change™ coins (items 74008, 74009, 73886),
T.E.A.M. Post-It® note cube (93337)

Step-by-step:

1. Fill a bowl with your choice of Cheerful Change coins. Bring the bowl and the Post-It cube to your next team meeting. Explain to the team that this is the bowl for "making change," and that the goal is to change to a more positive, helpful culture.

2. Explain to the team that whenever they see someone doing something that contributes to the team's goals, or helps a teammate, or makes things easier for a customer, they should write that person's name and what they did on a note and place it in the "Making Change" bowl. Then they take a coin from the bowl and give it to that co-worker, thanking them for the specific action that is making the workplace change for the better. Example: "You have demonstrated positive change for us by creating this customer service form, so I want to give some cheerful change to you."

3. When a team member receives a coin, he should look for someone else doing something helpful and pass it on, being sure to write what they did on a note and place it in the bowl.

4. When the bowl is empty of coins, celebrate with a lunch at the next team meeting. Ask everyone to bring back their coins to refill the bowl and begin again. When the coins are returned to the bowl, remove the Post-It notes and say, "Let's find out how we made change." Then ask everyone on the team to pick a note and read it. This allows them to re-live the helpful behavior and the recognition given for it.

This idea created by: Mike McCarthy • mikemccarthy@citcom.net

Chili Cook-off: Eat the Heat

Goal: Teambuilding and good eatin'.

Number of people: Unlimited.

Time: One long lunch hour.

Props: Award Board Plus (item 35123), chili-decorated certificates, badges for judges, aprons for chefs (they may bring their own or you may furnish).

Step-by-step:

1. Choose a date for a Chili Cook-off Contest. Publicize the date and invite all associates to submit entries in different categories, such as: Red and Green; Traditional and Non-Traditional; Red Meat, White Meat, No Meat; With Beans and No Beans.

2. Encourage entrants to bring their own favorite chef's aprons to wear during the whole workday just for fun.

3. Prepare all the "fixins."

4. Select lucky associates (based on a performance you want to recognize) to be judges, and ask them to wear badges.

5. Criteria for judging:
    a. Flavor
    b. Appearance
    c. Texture
    d. Aroma

6. Proclaim the category winners and designate all other entrants as runners-up to recognize them for their culinary contributions.

7. Write winners' names on certificates, mount on Award Boards, and present.

8. Pose all the chili chefs and judges for a smiling photo for your bulletin board and newsletter.

9. Eat the heat!

School News

Goal: Easy communication with students.

Number of people: Unlimited.

Time: 10 minutes.

Props: AwardMaker® software (item 13211 for Windows, 13212 for Mac).

Step-by-step:

1. To communicate quickly with all students or employees in your building, make a quick, attractive sign with AwardMaker.
2. Use bright colors and graphics to catch their busy eyes.
3. Post the signs next to wall clocks, for 100% viewership!
4. Additional uses:
   a. Class start and finish times
   b. Work schedules
   c. Awards for students
   d. Recognition for staff or employees

Created by: Bob Sconce • Fremont Middle School, Roseburg, OR

Trust and Teambuilding

Goal: Demonstrate how trust is gained or lost in a team.

Number of people: 3-20.

Time: 20 minutes.

Props: Flip chart and markers, Test 1 and Test 2 sheets (see Appendix, page 115), one per person.

Step-by-step:

1. Draw test 1 and test 2 on separate flip chart pages.
2. Make separate test sheets (8 ½" x 11") for 1 and 2, and distribute.
3. Show Test 1 and instruct the group using these exact words:

   a. "Put a dot on the 'I.'"

   b. "Write the word 'trust' in the spaces."

   c. "This is Mama Bull, Papa Bull, and Baby Bull. If Baby Bull gets sick, which parent will he go to? Circle your answer."

   d. "Circle the word that doesn't belong with the other three."

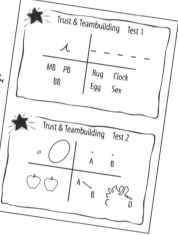

4. Ask them for their answers, then show correct answers by:

   a. Drawing a dot right on top of your vertical mark (not above it).

   b. Writing "trust" in the SPACES, not on the "underline" marks.

   c. Circling "Papa Bull." There's no such thing as "Mama Bull."

   d. Circling the word "sex." "You can beat a rug, a clock, an egg, but you can't beat sex."

5. Display Test 2 and give each person a copy. Instruct the group with these words:

   a. "On the left is a pea; on the right is a watermelon." Circle the larger one." Wait. You'll notice people hesitate to make a choice.

   b. "Draw a line from A to B." Wait. People will hesitate.

   c. "How many apples are there? Write your answer below."

   d. "Which line is longer: A to B, or C to D?" Hesitation.

6. Say, "The correct answers are the obvious ones; no tricks." Circle each answer.

7. Ask why they were reluctant to make choices. They'll respond with something like, "You tricked us! We've been burned." Discuss how this applies to trust in the team:

   a. "Once criticized for something, we won't take chances again."

   b. "How can we make sure this doesn't happen with our group?"

   c. "Do we 'catch' people doing something incorrect and point it out?"

   d. "What can we do instead?"

New Orleans Jazz Brunch for Teacher Motivation

Goal: Give teachers support and a boost with recognition, fun, and food.

Number of people: Limited only by the size of your cooking pots.

Time: 2-3 hours to prepare, 2 hours for fellowship and fun.

Props: Food, storyteller, Jazz band, tuxedo, evening dress, chef's hat or fancy apron, You Make the Difference Cheerful Change™ Coins (item 74009), Seeds of Praise (72733), tickets for door prizes, houseplants or other door prizes.

Step-by-step:

1. The week before an important event (such as state testing), invite teachers to a "Breakfast of Champions" New Orleans-style meal which you or a (really great) friend cook.

2. Ask parents to volunteer to fill in for teachers, giving them time off to attend.

3. Wear a tux or evening dress, or chef's hat or fancy apron.

4. Arrange for a jazz band to entertain.

5. Present teachers with Seeds of Praise, symbolizing the way teachers plant the seeds of knowledge in their students.

6. Invite a storyteller to entertain (The Rainbow Fish, a children's book about sharing, is a good one to read).

7. Tell the teachers how important their work is, and present them with a You Make the Difference coin.

8. Hold drawings for houseplants or other door prizes.

9. Listen, dance, eat, laugh.

This idea created by: Ralph Thibodeaux, Principal, and Elizabeth Gremillion, Assistant Principal Dozier Elementary School, Elrath, LA

The Maze

Goal: To teach the importance of cooperation over competition.

Number of people: 4 -12.

Time: 1 hour.

Props: 8' x 10' tarpaulin (preferably water-resistant material), duct tape (a color which contrasts with the color of the tarpaulin), noisemaker such as a tricycle a-ooga horn, and the maze solution (see Appendix, page 117).

Step-by-step:

1. Use duct tape to create "checkerboard" squares on one side of the tarp. Make 48 squares (8 x 6). Along the 10-foot edge of the tarpaulin, make 7 marks (left to right) at 17", 31", 45", 59", 73", 87", and 101". These become the "centers" for applying long strips of duct tape across the tarp.

   Along the 8-foot edge, repeat with 5 marks for applying tape. These do not need to be exact, and squares along outer borders will be a bit larger.

2. Make a copy of the following page to use as your "solution" to the maze.

3. Spread the tarp on the floor or grass and ask your group to gather around.

4. Explain that the goal is for every person to walk across the tarp, using the one and only path that will work, which only you know. They will have to figure out, by trial and error, one square at a time, the correct path. They may step only onto adjoining squares: forward, sideways, or backward. No diagonal steps and no skipping over squares. Participants may coach each other by using body language only. No talking. No "dropping breadcrumbs" or marking squares.

5. Explain that the first person will stand at the "narrow" (6-square) end of the tarp and begin by stepping on one of the squares. If she has picked the right square, she'll be allowed to stay on it and choose another square. If not, you honk the horn, and she steps backward off the tarp. Another person will try, then another, until someone gets the right square. When a person is "honked," he must step backward off the tarp, and another person try his exact path until she is "honked."

6. Once the entire correct path is discovered through trial and error, all other group members must travel the path correctly.

7. Give them 10 minutes to make a plan before silence is imposed.

8. Go! (It will take 10 to 25 minutes, depending on group size.)

9. After everyone is across, ask, "How would you have behaved differently if my instructions had been: 'First person across wins.'?"

10. Insights: Teamwork is helping others succeed, not trying to be best or first.

Off the Hook

Goal: When a co-worker makes a "good catch," learn to avoid shooting the messenger.

Number of people: 2
Time: 10 seconds.
Props: None.

Step-by-step:

1. To make sure you don't accidentally punish co-workers who come to inform you of problems (not whining: you, of course, know the difference); prepare some phrases to use when you respond to their news. Here are a few to get you started:

    a. "Good catch."

    b. "It's great that you told me so we can get crackin' on fixing it."

    c. "I'm so glad you're on top of this so early."

    d. _____

2. When a co-worker confesses his own mistake along with informing you of his plan to correct it, let him off the hook by letting him know he's not the only one who has ever made a mistake around here. Be sure to put your focus on the fact that he has caught the error and is taking the initiative to fix it. Sample supportive phrases (say them with a smile):

    a. "I hate it when I do that!"

    b. "I do that about once a week."

    c. "Now I know it's O.K. for me to make mistakes."

    d. "If that's the worst thing you do this week, you're a good guy!"

    e. _____

3. Your reward will come when your co-workers follow your lead and take care to let you off the hook when your time comes!

This idea created by: Janis Allen • janisallen@yahoo.com • www.janisallen.com

Talent Search

Goal: Find more qualities to appreciate about team members.
Number of people: 8-16.
Time: 15-30 minutes, depending on group size.
Props: Index cards, masking tape.

Step-by-step:

1. Distribute an index card to each person.

2. Ask them to think of a hidden talent they have. We're not looking for elaborate talents such as artists or musicians, but for "everyday" talents such as:
   Always on time, smile a lot, good listener, soccer coach, good with numbers, can fix things, have clean closets, is organized, makes great pies, etc.

3. Ask them to PRINT (to disguise handwriting) this talent on their card, keeping it hidden from others. Do not sign names.

4. Collect the cards, mix them up, and tape them around the wall.

5. Ask everyone to take a pen with him and walk around, looking at each card. They are to guess whose card each one is, and write the name of that person on the card. Everyone guesses on every card.

6. When all have written their guesses, ask everyone to stand next to their cards. Each person takes turns "coming clean," reading her talent, and telling the group how many people guessed correctly.

7. As leader of the group, make a card of your own, so you can join in the fun and share more fun facts about yourself.

8. You can do it again a week or two later, asking everyone to choose a different talent to reveal.

7 Ways to Get People to Meetings On Time

Goal: Create the culture of "on-time" meetings in your team.
Number of people: 7-21.
Time: 30 minutes.
Props: None.

Step-by-step:

1. As a kickoff when you form a team, or to create new "on-time" behaviors among your co-workers, lead this fun activity to create awareness of the importance of starting meetings on time for:
   a. Respecting others' time
   b. Time management
   c. Getting things done in meetings

2. Distribute copies of the following points:
   a. Start exactly on time, even if there's only one other person present. Become known for it.
   b. Close the door at start time.
   c. Distribute a concise agenda 48 hours before the meeting, including times set for each agenda item. Post it (large copy) in the meeting, and refer to it when you need to get back on track.
   d. Get into the agenda right away, with no more than 15 seconds of small talk.
   e. Put the most important agenda item, or most interesting news, first on the agenda.
   f. End the meeting at least one minute before the announced ending time.
   g. Schedule short meetings (30 minutes instead of an hour). Remember Parkinson's Law: "Work expands to fill the available time for its completion."

3. Ask individuals, pairs, or trios (depending on the number in your group) to select one of these seven points to:
   a. "Sell" to the rest of the group today (give 10 minutes to prepare).
   b. "Enforce" in future meetings with positive recognition when the on-time behaviors are exhibited, not just "zapping" for infractions.

4. After a few meetings, groups may switch to a different point for enforcing.

5. Celebrate your new on-time attendance with food and a humorous discussion of "the old days," before we became so famously "on time."

This idea created by: Janis Allen • janisallen@yahoo.com • www.janisallen.com

Follow the Money

Goal: Demonstrate the influence of positive recognition on success.
Number of people: 6-18.
Time: 30 minutes.
Props: Dollar bill.

Step-by-step:

1. Arrange seating in a circle or around a U-shaped table.
2. Ask a volunteer to leave the room, telling her that when she returns, she will be the hunter, to find a hidden object.
3. Ask the remaining group for ideas on where to hide a dollar bill, with the criteria that it be challenging but possible to find. Hide the dollar.
4. Instruct the remaining group that you want them to use three different responses to the hunter, in three one-minute time periods.

    a. First minute: do not look at the Hunter nor speak. Complete silence. Look at your shoes, close your eyes, stare at the floor, etc.

    b. Second minute: as the hunter moves around the room, say "cold" each time she moves further away from where the dollar is hidden. No mention of "warmer" during this minute.

    c. Third minute: say "warm" when she moves closer, and "cold" when she moves further away.

    d. Tell them you will signal them after each minute by walking across the room.

5. Bring the hunter in. Say, "We've hidden a dollar bill. Find it and it's yours.
6. After she finds it, lead a discussion with the group:

    a. Ask the hunter: "How did you feel during the first minute?" Second? Third?

    b. You may need to tell her what the group's instructions were, to help her sort out their responses during each minute.

    c. Ask the group, "How is this like working on a team?"

    d. "What happens when we don't get any feedback?"

    e. "How do we feel when we're told only when we're not on track (colder)?"

    f. "What happens to our ability to succeed when we're told both when we're off-track and when we're on track (warmer)?"

    g. "How does this (hearing both) affect our morale?"

    h. "In what situations in our department can we become better at giving each other 'warmer' feedback as well as 'colder'?"

This idea created by: Janis Allen • janisallen@yahoo.com • www.janisallen.com

Pat on the Back

Goal: Quickly give fun recognition to fellow team members.
Number of people: 25.
Time: 10 minutes.
Props: Paper, "non-bleed" markers, masking tape or clear tape.

Step-by-step:

1. At the end of a team or department meeting, ask each person to tape a piece of paper to his back.

2. Each team member takes a marker and writes something they appreciate about other team members on the papers on their backs, such as:

   a. A contribution the person made in the meeting

   b. A valuable contribution they've made to the team in the last two weeks

   c. A skill the person has

   d. An example of how she has helped co-workers

   e. _____

3. After the fun and laughter subsides, let everyone take their papers off and read them, or they can choose to leave them on their backs for other co-workers outside the team to see.

4. People are often pleasantly surprised by how their colleagues view them, and often discover overlooked talents in themselves!

5. Most people will post the papers at their desks or work stations for the world to see.

This idea created by: Glain Roberts-McCabe • Groberts@micaworld.com • MICA Seminars, Toronto, ON, Canada

The Hot Seat

Goal: Get to know members of a team.
Number of people: 16.
Time: 35 minutes.
Props: None.

Step-by-step:

1. One person acts as the timekeeper.
2. Each person takes a turn sitting in "the hot seat."
3. While in the "hot seat," other team members have two minutes to ask any question they want of the person sitting in that very warm chair.
4. Sample questions:
   a. "What's your favorite color?"
   b. "What's your favorite movie?"
   c. "When is your birthday?"
   d. "Do you have a significant other?"
   e. "What accomplishment are your most proud of?"
   f. "What's your most embarrassing moment?"
   g. _____

5. The person in the "hot seat" is allowed to say "Pass" to any question they're not comfortable answering.
6. The timekeeper calls "Time," or "Stop," or "Enough, already!" after two minutes.
7. The group may choose the guideline: "Everything that's shared will remain confidential."
8. Learn lot of information about fellow team members in a short time!

This idea created by: Elizabeth Peterson • epeterson@oxy.edu • Occidental College, Los Angeles, CA

Customer Service

CHAPTER 3

E-Mail Customer Service: Rude Dudes Revealed

Goal: Review professional e-mail etiquette for customer communication.

Number of people: 4 to 16.

Time: 30 minutes to 1hour, depending on group size.

Props: Flip chart paper, colored markers, masking tape, ePraise® base package.

Step-by-step:

1. Prepare a flip-chart page that looks like an e-mail screen, including To, From, Subject, and Text. Write a rude e-mail message to a customer on it, which would anger or confuse its recipient.

2. Post this sample, and tell the group that this is their big chance to write that rude e-mail they've always wanted to – without sending it, of course.

3. Ask for the group's input to help you edit your rude e-mail, so that you create a polite, clear, professional message which is the model for excellent customer communication. Use a contrasting color marker to mark through the rude words, then write the professional words above.

4. Assign pairs of team members to tape blank flip-chart sheets (one per pair) on the wall in separate corners. Spill out into halls or other rooms if needed for privacy.

5. Ask pairs to take 5 minutes to write their own rude or confusing e-mail, pulling no punches!

6. After 5 minutes, ask the pairs to walk to the message to their right, so that all pairs are now standing in front of another group's rude message.

7. Give each pair a marking pen in a contrasting color and ask them to edit (as you had demonstrated earlier), marking through the rude or confusing words, correcting the message by adding professional and helpful wording. Allow 5 minutes.

8. When all are finished, ask the whole group to gather around one message. Ask the pair who corrected it to read it aloud, first the original, then their correction. Then ask the whole group to walk to each one in turn. Enjoy hoots and hollers for this imaginary chance to be rude!

9. Back in REAL e-mail life, send ePraise notes to your customers for the things they do which make it easy to do YOUR job.

This idea created by: Janis Allen • janisallen@yahoo.com • www.janisallen.com

Stamp of Approval for Customer Service

Goal: Change the assumption that margin notes on a report means something's wrong.

Number of people: 2-10.

Time: 5 minutes to explain; 1 minute per person per day.

Props: Self-Inking stamps of approval, one per person; Thank U (item 75232); High Five (93515); Whatever It Takes (75067); Bravo (93514); You're a Shining Star (93346); You're the Best (75233); You Make the Difference (93516); Wow! (93345); T.E.A.M. (93344); You Rock (75066); Thank You (93343); Funky Stars (75234); Making the Difference border paper (23649); scissors.

Step-by-step:

1. Bring an assortment of self-inking stamps (one per person) to a team meeting.

2. Ask each person to select one stamp, which will become her individual "Stamp of Approval."

3. Ask each person over the next week to find something valuable (a behavior or result) in a report. Then she should circle it, pencil in a brief note as to why it is valuable, initial the note, and put her "Stamp of Approval" in the margin. Then deliver or send that report to the person responsible for that valuable behavior or result.

4. Everyone is asked to bring the stamped reports they received to next week's meeting, and read the identified behavior or result with its accompanying note and initials to the group.

5. The team leader brings scissors, cuts out each "Stamp of Approval" comment from the reports, and glues them on border paper to post on the bulletin board.

This idea created by: Janis Allen • janisallen@yahoo.com • www.janisallen.com

Put Yourself In Their Shoes

Goal: Help "phone" people and warehouse people appreciate what it takes for the opposite group to do their jobs (can be used during Customer Service Week).

Number of people: 2-50.

Time: 2 hours to prepare; 5 minutes per participant during the day.

Props: Tagboard (poster paper) "Telephone Gal" and "Warehouse Guy" cutouts, extra pre-cut smaller pieces of tagboard, scissors, crayons, and tape.

Step-by-step:

1. Ahead of time, make two silhouettes of people with tagboard, one male and one female, 30" to 60" tall. Attach these figures to some kind of panel (such as a small erasable board or anything to provide support). Set them on top of a banquet table or smaller table in a high-traffic area convenient to both customer service and warehouse associates.

2. On the table, provide smaller pieces of tagboard on which you've drawn outlines of the tools each group needs to do their jobs. You'll ask participants to "finish" the pieces by cutting them out and coloring them.

   Draw items like pens, clip boards, tool boxes, headsets, a computer mouse, packing boxes, etc. to give participants ideas. Provide plenty of extra pieces of small tagboard for participants to use to create extra items.

3. Explain to the groups that you want them to think of all the tools and items it takes for the opposite group to do their jobs, to increase awareness and appreciation of the other group.

4. Ask everyone to stop by the table today and create or "finish" a tool for the opposite group's silhouette, and tape it to the silhouette.

5. Encourage groups to participate that day, as these new paper employees will be completed and displayed for everyone tomorrow!

This idea created by: Amy Rohrbach • amyr@baudville.com • www.baudville.com

ePraise International

Goal: Personalize customer and vendor relationships around the world.
Number of people: Unlimited.
Time: One minute per day.
Props: ePraise® software (item 15024).

Step-by-step:

1. As you communicate with your vendors, suppliers, or customers on the phone or via e-mail, take a moment as you become comfortable to find out a bit about them as individuals.

2. When it's appropriate, ask, "What's going on in your life?" or any form of question you're comfortable with that signals, "I see you as a person."

3. Learn about their new grandchildren, children's graduations, marriages, deaths, promotions, new homes, new cars, softball leagues, church events, etc.

4. Immediately after this communication, and before you forget, send the person an ePraise to extend the appropriate feelings.

5. Now enjoy their pleasantly surprised reactions.

Created by: Judy Brady • BradyJudy@otc.army.mil • DynCorp, a CSC Corporation

Customer Service Do's & Don'ts

Goal: Refresh your group's memories on good and bad customer practices.

Number of people: 2-20.

Time: 30 minutes.

Props: Flip chart and markers, index cards, hat, small box or basket.

Step-by-step:

1. Tape two flip-chart sheets side-by-side on a wall. Ask for two volunteers to be writers. Ask one to write "Good" at the top of their sheet, and the other to write "Bad" at the top of theirs.

2. Distribute two index cards to everyone else in the group.

3. Ask them to think of their worst experience as a customer and write a few key words describing it on one of the index cards, then sign their names.

4. Ask them to do the same with their best experience as a customer on another card.

5. Ask them to put both cards in the hat.

6. Draw a card from the hat, read the key words aloud, then ask its author to tell the story in one minute. It's important to keep these short; we can all talk forever about our bad experiences.

7. Just before each person begins to tell his story, ask the group to see how quickly they can tell whether this is a "good customer service" or "bad customer service" story – like identifying a song after hearing only a few notes.

8. When someone wants to guess, she may raise her hand, the person telling the story will pause, and the guesser will say, "Good" or "Bad."

9. The storyteller will confirm the guess, then ask the person at the flip chart sheet to listen to the story and capture the key behaviors of the customer service (or sales) person which makes this a "Good" or a "Bad" story. She'll write those key behaviors (words or short phrases) on the paper.

10. Continue to draw cards out and repeat the steps above until all are drawn.

11. Discuss what the "bad" stories have in common.

12. Discuss what the "good" stories have in common.

13. Save the flip chart sheets to post in your department or review at your next meeting.

This idea created by: Janis Allen • janisallen@yahoo.com • www.janisallen.com

Listen to the Customer

Goal: Overcoming barriers to listening when on the phone with customers.

Number of people: 8-24.

Time: One hour.

Props: 8 different colors of 8 ½ x 11" paper, 8 clear plastic sheet protectors, 8 sheets of card stock (8 ½ x 11"), 2 toy telephone receivers or headsets.

Step-by-step:

1. Prepare title cards on colored paper by printing the following titles in large font (landscape-oriented), one per sheet.
   a. Noisy work space
   b. Fatigue or stress
   c. Customer speaks too slowly or too much
   d. Visual distractions/Co-workers trying to get my attention
   e. Customer speaks fast or with accent
   f. Customer is unclear or uses terms I don't know
   g. Customer raises voice or speaks rudely
   h. I think I know what the customer is going to say
2. Put each title card into a sheet protector with a sheet of card stock.
3. Ask your group to stand in a circle.
4. Explain that on each card is a barrier to good listening. Many of these we can't control, but we can figure out some ways to deal with them professionally and listen effectively.
5. Read each one to the group, then toss it onto the floor in the center.
6. When all eight are on the floor, ask everyone to select the card he'd like to work on. (You may have one, two, or three people per card.)
7. Ask them to take the title cards and go to separate places in the room.
8. Ask them to prepare a short skit for the group, with one person playing the role of the customer and one person playing the role of the customer service representative, to include:
   a. Introducing their topic by reading and holding up the title card
   b. Using the phones or headsets, acting out:
      i. The wrong way to react when this barrier is present
      ii. The right way to react when this barrier is present
9. After each group finishes, display their title cards at the front of the room.
10. Use the eight cards as your visual aids to summarize the key points learned during these dramatic moments.

This idea created by: Janis Allen · janisallen@yahoo.com · www.janisallen.com

Vocal Charades for Customer Service

Goal: Fine-tune your voice for a professional phone personality.
Number of people: 5-20.
Time: 45 minutes.
Props: Flip chart or erasable board and markers, five Index cards.

Step-by-step:

1. Write the five voice qualities below on your chart paper or board, and also on index cards (one per card).
   a. Tone: expresses feeling, the "smile" in your voice.
   b. Inflection: emphasizing words to express meaning
   c. Pitch: how high or low voice sounds
   d. Rate: number of words spoken per minute
   e. Volume: how loud or soft voice sounds

2. If you have more than five people, divide your group into five small groups (2, 3, or 4 per group).

3. Fold the cards to conceal what's written on them, and put them into a hat or basket.

4. Ask each group to draw a card. This becomes their subject for Vocal Charades.

5. Without letting the other groups know which card they have drawn, they are asked to create a charade with their voices (one or several persons can speak; it's their call). The purpose of the charade is to demonstrate the extremes of the voice quality on the card they've drawn. They will act out the charade with their voices. They should keep their backs to the group, so facial expressions won't be seen.

6. As each group acts its charade, the other groups guess which of the five voice qualities is being demonstrated.

7. When someone guesses correctly, stop and discuss the impression we make on customers with the tone, inflection, pitch, rate, or volume of our voices.

8. Ask each person to choose one voice quality she would like to fine-tune in her conversations with customers.

This idea created by: Janis Allen • janisallen@yahoo.com • www.janisallen.com

Cheerful Change is Cool at the Pool

Goal: Reward outstanding customer service.

Number of people: Unlimited.

Time: 10 seconds per person recognized.

Props: Cheerful Change™ coins (item 73886).

Step-by-step:

1. Provide managers with a jar of Cheerful Change to keep in their offices.
2. Ask them to look for times when a summer aquatics program employee goes out of her way to:
   a. Do work that is "extra"
   b. Spend extra time to teach a customer effectively
   c. Make a staff member feel more comfortable and needed
   d. Implement a new idea
3. Coach them to tell those individuals that they appreciate what the summer employee did, referring to the particular action recognized, and then to hand out a Cheerful Change coin.
4. Employees may then redeem the coins for:
   a. Food or drinks at the snack bar
   b. An extra break
   c. One "get-out-of-an-assignment-free"
5. Cheerful Change is extremely cost effective, since the coins are redeemed for the reward of choice, then used again, and again!

This idea created by: Sharon Mahany Brooks • Community Services Department, Rocklin, CA

Customer Window

Goal: Learn how you can better serve your internal customers.

Number of people: 1-30.

Time: 20 minutes per customer response.

Props: Customer Window sheets (see Appendix, page 119), one per customer you wish to survey.

Step-by-step:

1. Create Customer Window sheets by drawing two lines to divide an 8 ½ x 11" sheet in four quadrants. Label each quadrant with the information you're asking for in each box:

    a. What you want and get from me (or my department)

    b. What you want but don't get

    c. What you get but don't want

    d. What you don't want and don't get

2. Visit your internal customers privately, one-by-one. Tell them that you would like to have 20 minutes to find out how you can serve them better.

3. Explain the Customer Window sheet and how it will help you. Ask for information from them in either of two ways:

    a. Interview them during this meeting and fill in the boxes with their responses, or leave it with them if they prefer to have time to think about it and complete it on their own. Tell them when you would like them to return it and jot the date down on the form.

    b. When you receive their responses, whether verbally or on paper, take care to be open and non-defensive about any criticism you receive. Your customers will tell you some things that you may not find easy to hear. It's important not to argue, justify why you do things the way you do them now, or be defensive in any way. You're not obligated to make all the changes they ask for. Just write them down and tell your customer that you'll think about these and respond by a certain date. Thank them for taking time to give you their ideas.

4. Use the information from quadrants B and C to plan improvements you can make.

5. Feel good about the information you get in quadrants A and D. This is what your customer likes about your work!

6. Options:

    a. A supervisor may use it to learn what her team would like from her.

    b. Team members may use it with each other if there is strong trust.

7. If you're not in an open, non-defensive mood, don't use this tool. Save it until you're ready to listen to negative feedback and receive it as an opportunity to improve.

This idea reported by: Janis Allen • janisallen@yahoo.com • www.janisallen.com

Happy Bedfellows

Goal: Recognize outstanding hospital patient care.

Number of people: Unlimited.

Time: 5 minutes per person recognized.

Props: ePraise® (item 15024), Celebrating Excellence certificate paper (22054), Outstanding Achievement certificate seals (62996), AwardMaker® software (13569 for Windows, 13570 for Mac).

Step-by-step:

1. To give extra recognition to employees who receive positive comments, verbal or written, from patients or their families, equip all your department managers and supervisors with tools to make recognition easy and lasting.

    a. Use ePraise software for quick e-mail notes the employees can print, save, and take home to put on the refrigerator.

    b. Make certificates to be presented at your management council meetings.

    c. Add a personal gift such as a plant, gift certificate, CD, or book for performances that go above and beyond.

2. Use these tools to double the impact of recognition received from happy patients. Employees get recognized once by the patient, then again by their manager. This lets them know how important their good work is!

These ideas created by:
James Phillips • JLPhillips@lakelandregional.org • Lakeland Medical Center, St, Joseph, MI
Carole Berger • CVBerger@drmc.org • DuBois Regional Medical Center, DuBois, PA
Eileen O'Hare • Eileen.Ohare@cchmc.org • Cincinnati Children's Hospital and Medical Center, Cincinnati, OH
Elaine M. Olin • eolin@cms.hhs.gov • Centers for Medicare and Medicaid Services, Baltimore, MD

Customer Relationship Management - Bank On It!

Goal: Manage relationships with your best/most valued customers.

Number of people: Unlimited.

Time: 2 hours per week.

Props: You Make the Difference coupon set (item 75045), pocket folder (35030), and Mints (93160); Together We Can Make a Difference poster (73994); Events recognition board with stickers (73673); Making the Difference totebags (94010), Pens (73965), Tumblers (93971), and Mouse Pads (93972); books from the Baudville Recognition Library, Presentation FUNdamentals™ PowerPoint™ backgrounds (13983); Baudville Software Suite (13730); ePraise® online e-card recognition tool (15024).

Step-by-step:

1. Prepare a PowerPoint presentation use the Making the Difference background from Presentation FUNdamentals software to give examples of customer relationship management and train your entire employee group.

2. Print event materials and recognition using software suite.

3. Introduce Customer Relationship Management to all employees with a kickoff to form teams. Everyone from couriers to the president and board of directors are on teams.

4. Introduce your focus on Quality Customer Service for your best/most valued customers.

5. Give out pocket folders, pens, and mints to all employees. Have drawings for mousepads, tumblers, and totebags.

6. For added fun, ask your male executives to dress up as women, women to dress as men, and lip-synch "We Are Family."

7. Give posters, recognition boards and books to team leaders. Ask them to have daily 5-minute huddles to cover the topic of the day, educate, and give recognition.

8. Equip managers with coupon sets for special recognition.

9. Give ePraise software to ALL employees for great peer recognition.

10. This page won't hold all the good ideas! Please e-mail Patti for more info.

This idea created by: Patti Leopard • PLeopard@georgiabankandtrust.com
Georgia Bank & Trust Company of Augusta, Augusta, GA

Good Impressions for Customer Service

Goal: Understand the impression you make on others and refine customer skills.
Number of people: 8 to 32.
Time: 20 - 30 minutes.
Props: Lists of scenarios such as listed in step 5 below (1 copy per 4-6 people).

Step-by-step:

1. Divide group into teams of 4-6. (Number off to separate people who are most familiar with each other.)
2. Ask teams to select a leader who will best succeed in the scenarios you will give them. Participants cannot ask about the experiences or expertise of their team members; selection is based only on their observations of this person's behavior and how she appears.
3. The same person can be selected as leader for two or more scenarios.
4. At the end of the selection phase, a team representative will be asked to explain to the entire group why each selection was made.
5. Sample scenarios (revise according to your organization's challenges):
   Who do you think would lead this team to:
   a. Find our way out of the woods at night?
   b. Meet extremely challenging customer retention/sales goals?
   c. Escape a snarling dog?
   d. Apologize to irate customers and save the business?
   e. Calm a crying lost child?
   f. Finish a complex, important report within three hours?
   g. Plan the 50th annual company picnic?
   h. Sell 1,000 tickets for a local charity concert?
   i. Remain patient when being blamed?
6. These scenarios are meant to indicate how appearance, facial expression, voice, posture, willingness to act, etc., project definable impressions on co-workers and customers.
7. Read the first scenario out loud, then ask each team's spokesperson to name the leader they selected and explain why the group selected him.
8. On a flip chart or erasable board, ask someone to record the qualities which influenced the team to select that person. Ask the teams to be very specific with their comments, so that everyone gets a clear picture of the qualities which are perceived as successful.
7. Read the other scenarios in turn to complete all your scenarios.
9. Capture the qualities listed and review with the group quarterly.
10. Give lots of recognition when you see people exhibit these qualities!

This idea created by: Madrid Zimmerman • Madrid_aparc@citcom.net • Al Platt Architect, PA

Money in the Bank

Goal: In banking, increase referrals from all associates to bankers.
Number of people: Unlimited.
Time: 1 minute per person recognized.
Props: Balloons in assorted colors.

Step-by-step:

1. When any bank associate refers a customer to a banker for additional services, have the banker inflate a balloon and place it on that person's desk or countertop.

2. Take a deep breath and prepare to inflate lots of colorful balloons when associates see what's happening!

This idea created by: BK Myers • bnkrsings@aol.com • Wells Fargo Bank, Grover Beach, CA

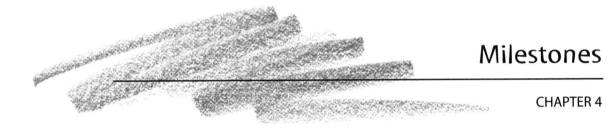

Milestones

Soft Landing: Welcome New Associates

Goal: Make new people in your department feel welcome and valued.
Number of people: 1 to 30.
Time: 5 minutes to organize, then 2 minutes per person per week for 3 weeks.
Props: T.E.A.M. certificate paper (item 23476WT), Post-it® cubes (93337), mouse pad (93458), T.E.A.M. Bundle (75228).

Step-by-step:

1. The day before a new person joins your department, pass a "Welcome to our Team" certificate around, inviting each person to write a welcome note and sign it.

2. Put the certificate into the gift bag (from the T.E.A.M. bundle). Add the mouse pad and the new person's own supply of theme Post-it notes.

3. Distribute theme Post-it notes to department members.

4. Ask each person, the day after the new person begins work, to begin writing Post-it recognition notes, naming something specific they value about the way the new associate is doing his or her work.

5. Each person is asked to secretly stick her Post-it note on the bottom of the new person's mouse pad, which is on the new person's desk.

6. Ask people to volunteer to do this on a certain day of the week, so that notes are distributed throughout the new person's first three weeks.

7. Tell the new person that his mouse will occasionally be delivering new "mousepad mail" for him, and he may want to check under his pad every few days.

8. Each person is asked to stop by the new person's work area at least twice during the three weeks to ask about his "mouse pad mail." This gives the new person the opportunity to share his recognition notes, and feel good all over again!

Anniversary Month

Goal: Affirm the work of a co-worker in his first month.

Number of people: 3-15.

Time: 15 minutes;

Props: Funky Stars pop-up Pocket Praise® cards (item 75310), You make a world of difference Squeezable Praise™ ball (93125).

Step-by-step:

1. Ask all co-workers of the person who is marking his first month in your department to write Pocket Praise cards to the new person, naming one way that person has made a difference to the team.

2. Ask everyone to attend a 10-minute meeting on the new person's one-month anniversary.

3. Stand in a circle.

4. As leader, holding the Squeezable Praise ball in your hand, read your Pocket Praise note aloud. Give the note to the person, then toss the ball to someone else around the circle. That person reads her note, gives it to the new person, and tosses the ball, until everyone has had a turn.

5. When everyone is finished, toss the ball to the honoree to keep as a reminder of this celebration.

Created by: Gail Hahn, MA, CSP, CPRP, CLL • gail@funcilitators.com • www.funcilitators.com

Anniversary Food and Fun

Goal: Honor individuals who are marking company anniversary dates that month.
Number of people: Unlimited.
Time: One long lunch hour.
Props: Anniversary Lapel Pins (item 75617, indicate year 1 - 20).

Step-by-step:

1. Each month, invite all the associates whose company anniversary date falls into that month to a special lunch to honor them.

2. Invite the executive management team to socialize and eat with the honoree's.

3. Have everyone sit around one big table.

4. For a great way to get to know each other, ask people to volunteer answers to these questions:

    a. What is your favorite memory working here?

    b. What was your most embarrassing moment?

    c. What accomplishment in your life are you most proud of?

    d. Tell us something unique about your hometown.

    e. What's one thing you haven't yet experienced in life, but would like to?

    f. What's your most cherished childhood memory?

    g. If you had a chance to do one thing in your life, with no boundaries, what would that be?

5. Ask each honoree's manager to present him with an Anniversary Lapel Pin.

Add Sparkle to Awards Meetings

Goal: Make special meetings coordinated, professional, and fun.
Number of people: Unlimited.
Time: 2 hours.
Props: Starlight border paper (item 22709), Gift Certificate (25199),
Jumbo Postcard (22880), and Adhesive Labels (43009) – or create your own
with Event FUNdamentals (13703).

Step-by-step:

1. Print and send invitations to invitees using colorful border paper.
2. Make table signs to designate seating arrangements, or to carry your slogan for the meeting (use jumbo postcard stock).
3. Create festive nametags by printing names on adhesive labels.
4. Add flowers, crepe paper streamers, or balloons to tables to complement your paper colors.
5. Create awards using gift certificate letter paper, which:
   a. Reminds you and your colleagues to give written explanations of the performance your recipients demonstrated to earn awards, and
   b. Makes "gifting" easy with the use of perforated gift certificates
6. Recipients tear off the lower portion of their awards and redeem them for the awards you offer, such as:
   a. A car wash
   b. Movie tickets
   c. Meal tickets
   d. Gasoline gift certificates
   e. One hour off with pay
   f. Reserved parking for one week
   g. Fresh flowers on your desk
   h. Supervisor brings you coffee (or other) every morning for one week
   i. Manicure
   j. Massage
   k. _____

This idea created by: Pamela Murray • pamelam@fws.com • ABC Fine Wine & Sprits, Orlando, FL

Sweet Anniversary

Goal: Recognize a co-worker's company anniversary.

Number of people: Unlimited.

Time: 30 minutes.

Props: Banana split ingredients, Pocket Praise® cards (item 73926, etc.), balloons, colored napkins, plastic bowls, spoons, ice-cream scoops.

Step-by-step:

1. To celebrate the company anniversary of a co-worker, distribute Pocket Praise cards ahead of time, and invite the honoree's current and past co-workers to write "What I value about your service to our organization" messages to the honoree. Ask everyone to bring their Pocket Praise cards to the party.

2. Find a very old photo of the honoree, enlarge it, and post it in the party room.

3. Decorate the room and assemble the ingredients for banana splits.

4. Invite individuals to volunteer to read their cards aloud to the honoree (this makes speech giving easy and short). Of course, many people may prefer to keep their messages private.

5. Ask everyone to give the Pocket Praise cards to the honoree.

6. Invite the honoree to be first in line to build her own sweet treat.

7. Take plenty of candid photos during the event, and then give them to the honoree later.

8. Forget those diets and enjoy!

Birthday Blurbs

Goal: Make a co-worker laugh on her birthday.

Number of people: Unlimited.

Time: 2 minutes per birthday person .

Props: ePraise® e-card recognition (item 15024).

Step-by-step:

1. Create a variety of personalized, funny, or silly "blurbs" on your ePraise e-cards which you can send to co-workers celebrating birthdays.

2. Below each one, write a personal note saying something special about the individual.

3. Here's one "blurb" idea:

   Happy birthday to you

   Happy birthday to you

   Happy birthday, dear _____

   Happy birthday to youuuuuuuuuuuuuuuuuuuu

   I thought you would appreciate the fact that I sent this via e-mail rather than singing it!

   Have a great birthday. Best wishes, _____

This idea created by: Mike Pancoe and Ellie Liberty • First Data Corp., Omaha, NB

PayNotes

Goal: Mark a special occasion for an individual.

Number of people: 2 (you and one other).

Time: 10 seconds.

Props: Paycheck with stub, pen.

Step-by-step:

1. Before giving or sending a check to an associate or vendor, write a brief celebratory or congratulatory mini-message on the check stub.

2. Use this idea for checks to associates within your organization, or to vendors you're comfortable with.

3. To associates:

   a. "Welcome!" for a new associate

   b. "What a week!" for someone who's been really stretched

   c. "Your sixth month!" to mark an anniversary

   d. "Hello there, Ms. Team Leader" to mark a promotion

   e. "Whew! You did it." when a large project is completed

   f. _____

4. To vendors:

   a. "Here we go" for the beginning of a new project or contract

   b. "It's easy to do business with you" to a vendor who has earned this

   c. "Thanks for your quick reaction time" for fast help

   d. "Hey there, partner" to a long-time excellent supplier

   e. _____

5. The receiver of this check will get a smile and a good feeling about your business relationship in addition to money for his checking account!

This idea created by: Debra Sikanas • debras@baudville.com • www.baudville.com

Red, White, and Blue

Goal: Create a patriotic theme for a special event.

Number of people: Unlimited.

Time: 2 days to plan, 90 minutes to enjoy.

Props: Stars & Stripes border paper (item 21077), Trifold (22618), Name Badges (42669); T.E.A.M. Flag certificate holders (35029); red, white, and blue balloons; red and blue ribbon; T.E.A.M. Flag buttons (73881) or T.E.A.M. Flag t-shirts (93560).

Step-by-step:

1. Use theme papers to create a patriotic look for special events, such as:
   a. Welcoming a new employee (especially if the person is a former military employee)
   b. Celebrating goal achievement of a department or total company
   c. Annual meeting
   d. Quality conference where teams present project results
   e. Installation of officers
   f. _____

2. Use Stars & Stripes border paper to issue invitations.

3. Decorate tables with balloons and ribbons.

4. Put a round cake (already sliced) in center of table for dessert.

5. Make signs to put on tables (using Stars & Stripes trifold) to show:
   a. Seating designations, or
   b. Your organization's Vision Statement, or
   c. Today's meeting theme

6. Place agendas or menus inside T.E.A.M. Flag certificate holders and place on table. Give holders as meeting keepsake.

7. Attach one T.E.A.M. Flag button to each holder, which people may remove and wear, or place T.E.A.M. Flag t-shirts, in assorted sizes, on welcome table with stacks of sizes marked. Invite everyone to select one.

8. Print names of attendees on Stars & Stripes name badges, and place on the welcome table for individuals to pick up when they arrive.

9. Invite a speaker from a nearby military base, if possible.

10. Invite a brass band to entertain with marches and patriotic songs (a high school R.O.T.C. drill team or color guard may perform free!).

This idea created by: Paula Filer • pFiler@tampabayrealtor.com • Pinellas REALTOR Organization, St. Petersburg, FL

"You Make the Difference" Retirement Party

Goal: Celebrate the professional achievements of a co-worker who is retiring.

Number of people: Unlimited.

Time: 8 hours preparation, 2 hours for the party.

Props: You Make the Difference: border paper (item 23276), trifold (24027), quarter-size notepad (25168), celebration tumbler (93352), gift basket (94054), chrome star photo frame (95194); snap-together buttons (41181).

Step-by-step:

1. Invite all current and former co-workers of your retiring friend to a dinner or lunch, using You Make the Difference border paper for the invitations. Explain that the party's theme will be to let the honoree know how he has made a difference to this organization and its people.

2. With the invitation, enclose 2-3 sheets from the You Make the Difference quarter-size notepad. Ask the attendees to write a note to the honoree on one or more of these sheets, mentioning something specific he has done which has made the difference to them, and sign their names. Ask them to bring these sheets with them to the party.

3. Arrange ahead of time for "toasters" and "roasters."

4. Find a recent picture of your honoree at work (posed with co-workers if available) and frame it in the You Make the Difference chrome star frame.

5. In secret, ask a relative of your retiring co-worker to give you a photo of the person from younger days – high school, perhaps. Enlarge or reduce the size of the face on the photo to fit nicely in 3" snap-together buttons. Make enough buttons for each party attendee, plus 6 extra for the honoree (he'll enjoy giving them to his family later).

6. Give the buttons to attendees ahead of time and ask them to wear them. Your honoree will be quite surprised to find his face from years gone by on everyone's chest!

7. Print the party program on jumbo post cards and place one at each person's place at the table.

8. When guests arrive, ask them to place their p  Make the Difference celebration tumbler, wh the framed photo and gift basket.

This idea created by: Janis Allen • janisallen@yahoo.com • www.janisallen.com

Retirement: Pocket Praise Goes Public

Goal: To recognize individuals who have served on your team
or board and are moving on.

Number of people: Limited to who is on your team or board.

Time: 5 minutes to prepare cards; about 15-20 minutes for the ceremony.

Props: Thank You assortment Pocket Praise® cards (item 72809),
You Make a Difference gift basket (94054).

Step-by-step:

1. Select an individual who has completed her role on your team
   or your board of directors.

2. In advance of the recognition ceremony, distribute one Pocket Praise card
   to every member of your team or board who worked with this individual.
   Ask them to complete the card before the meeting.

3. At the recognition ceremony, ask the honoree to sit in a prominent
   place in front of the gift basket.

4. Tell a story about her that recalls a memorable experience you have
   had with him or her.

5. Ask her to share what she has gained or found most enjoyable about
   working on this team or board.

6. One by one, invite the team or board members to present their
   Pocket Praise cards, either reading the content out loud, or just adding
   the card to the gift basket.

7. Present the gift basket and cards. Ask for a standing ovation.

This idea created by: Lois Hart, Ed.D. • lhart@seqnet.net
Executive Director, Women's Leadership Institute, Denver CO

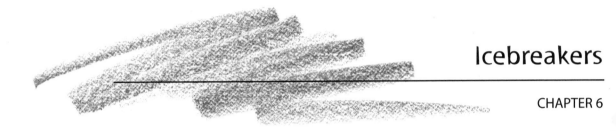

Icebreakers

CHAPTER 6

"All the Dirt" Bingo

Goal: Warm up the group.
Number of people: 6 to 20.
Time: 15-30 minutes, depending on the number in the group.
Props: You Rock jumbo postcards: one per person (item 25104).

Step-by-step:

1. Create a bingo card graphic of 16 blocks. In each block, print humorous or interesting personal information such as "received speeding ticket," "own red shoes," "worked here for more than 5 years," "have more than one pet," etc. If you're stuck for ideas, see Baudville's poster "Extraordinary" (item 33551). Leave one square blank.

2. Print your bingo cards on You Rock postcards.

3. Give each person a bingo card.

4. Ask them to PRINT a secret attribute or personal fact in the blank square (so their handwriting can't be identified).

5. Take back all the cards, shuffle them, and deal them out again. If anyone gets his own card, take back five cards, shuffle, and give them back until no one has his own card.

6. Instruct participants to walk around the room, talking to each other to find out who "fits" each square, and writing that person's name into the square on her own bingo card.

7. Call time after 10, 15, or 20 minutes, depending on the size of your group.

8. Ask each to count and report the number of names they've written on their cards, and add them on a board or flip chart as they report. Total the numbers and humorously celebrate the all the "dirt" we now know about each other!

Hats Off to You!

Goal: Warm up a group or create fun on a special day.

Number of people: 4-20.

Time: 20 minutes.

Props: Paper hats folded from 11"x17" sheets of paper (see Appendix, page 121), crayons and markers, scissors, colored paper, glue, tape, feathers, ribbons, or anything colorful and fun which might be glued to a paper hat.

Step-by-step:

1. Prepare hat "templates" by folding 11"x17" sheets of paper into hats that can be decorated and worn. You'll need one per person.

2. Write the names of all participants on pieces of paper and put into a hat.

3. Ask each person to draw a name, then decorate a hat for the person whose name he drew. Ask him to decorate that hat with symbols or words which symbolize that person's strengths or skills. Fun things about the person can also be included.

4. People may return to their work areas to make their concoctions in secret.

5. Ask everyone to deliver the hat she made to her secret partner when it's finished.

6. Everyone wears his hat all day for a day that's filled with smiles.

This idea created by: Amy Rohrbach • amyr@baudville.com • www.baudville.com

Stress Person

Goal: When stress in your organization is unusually high, don't just break the ice, melt it!

Number of people: 4 to 20.

Time: 15 minutes .

Props: Flip chart paper, four or more colors of marking pens, masking tape, Squeezable Praise™ stress shapes (You shine! item 92902; You Make the Difference 73925; You Are a Star, 75411).

Step-by-step:

1. Ask the group to count off 1-4. Ask all "ones" to congregate in one corner, "two's" in another, and so forth.

2. Ask each group to tape four sheets of flip chart paper together to form a rectangle which will roughly accommodate a human body lying on it, with his arms extended to the side.

3. Ask that one person in each group volunteer to be the artist's model, who will allow another member (the artist) to trace the outline of his body on the paper. The group can either tape the paper to the wall and have the model stand against it, or put it on the floor and have the model lie on it.

4. When the body is drawn, the paper is taped to the wall, and each group member draws a symbol on the body in the place where she physically feels stress (hammer in head, knot in stomach, sweat on brow, etc.).

5. When finished, take turns having the whole group visit each Stress Person, and ask that group's members to point out his or her stress symbol and explain:

   a. What she feels

   b. What triggers this feeling

6. Give a Squeezable Praise stress toy to each person to help him relieve his stress.

7. Keep the art on the wall for the duration of the meeting, and keep adding to it for fun.

Created by: Michael McCarthy • mikemccarthy@citcom.net

95

Sole Mate Search

Goal: Introductions and icebreaker.
Number of people: 6-30.
Time: 10 - 20 minutes (depending on group size).
Props: Flip chart or erasable board and marker.

Step-by-step:

1. Ask everyone to stand up and move to an open space in the room where it's large enough to make a circle.

2. Tell the group they now have the chance in a lifetime to find their Sole Mates. Write "Sole Mate" on the flip chart or board. Ask if they notice anything unusual about the way it's spelled. Ask them to guess what this means.

3. Tell them that you want them to look around the circle and find a pair of shoes that either:
   a. Is similar to theirs, or
   b. They'd like to own

4. Ask them to walk to the person wearing those shoes and then, together, find a quiet corner somewhere in the room to talk.

5. Write them a list (on your flipchart or board) of facts to find out about their Sole Mates, such as (select only three from below, to keep it brief):
   a. Name
   b. Nickname
   c. Job title
   d. Job they had before this one
   e. What do you like most/dislike most about your work?
   f. What's your hobby?

6. Give them a total of 5 minutes to interview each other, and ask them to be ready to reveal all about their Sole Mate when time is up.

7. Have Sole Mates introduce each other, then return to seats.

8. Variation: Later in the day, if you want to do an exercise using four people per group, you can ask them all to stand with their Sole Mates again, and ask each pair to team up with another Sole Mate pair based on (select one):
   a. These four pairs of shoes would make a complete wardrobe, or
   b. These four pairs of shoes could be best friends, or
   c. These four pairs of shoes were bought at about the same time

This idea refined by: Marianne Frederick • MFredck@aol.com • WorkPlay, Inc. Taylors, SC

Picture This

Goal: Get to know other people in a fun way.
Number of people: 6 to 20.
Time: 10-20 minutes, depending on the number in the group.
Props: Paper and pencils.

Step-by-step:

1. Ask participants to draw three pictures, one on each of three sheets of paper, depicting three of their favorite things to do (keeping them hidden).

2. Ask them to turn all three sheets face down, then, picking up the one on top, walk around the room showing the picture to several other people, asking them to guess what this drawing reflects.

3. Call time after 10 minutes and ask everyone to pick up the second drawing and repeat.

4. Call time after 5 minutes and ask everyone to pick up their third drawing and repeat.

5. Call time after 5 minutes, ask everyone to be seated, and debrief by asking the group the most surprising things they learned about their co-workers.

Energizers

CHAPTER 7

Life Raft

Goal: Energize a group with a physical activity.

Number of people: 2-8.

Time: 5 minutes.

Props: Tarpaulin 5' by 8' or larger.

Step-by-step:

1. Ask all members of your group to stand on the tarp. Tell them that they are shipwrecked, but they have managed to climb aboard this raft.

2. Explain that stepping off the raft means to step into the ocean and drown. The side which now faces down is a silver reflective material which will attract the rescue plane.

3. Their goal is to turn the tarp completely over while keeping all members' feet on the tarp.

4. If anyone steps off the tarp, it must be returned to its original position and the group must start again.

5. More difficult variation: only feet, not hands, can be used to turn the tarp.

ABC: A Bit of Conversation

Goal: Energize a group and teach them to let go of outcomes, going with the flow.

Number of people: 6-26.

Time: 15 minutes.

Props: Only a memory of the alphabet is needed!

Step-by-step:

1. Ask your group to stand in a circle.

2. Explain that you will begin a nonsense conversation by making a statement or asking a question with a word that begins with the letter "A." You may choose a topic that's relevant to your business, or choose a funny, non-work topic.

3. The person to your right will then respond to your statement or question with her own sentence, using a word that begins with "B."

4. The person to her right will respond using "C" to begin his sentence, and so on to "Z," going around two or three times if needed. Pity the poor folks who end up with X and Z.

5. De-brief with these questions:

    a. How did it feel when someone skipped a letter?

    b. How did it feel when someone changed the topic inside the flow?

    c. What can we learn from this about how we react to the unknown?

6. Return to your seats with new alpha-energy and insights!

This idea created by: Gail Hahn, MA, CSP, CPRP, CLL • gail@funcilitators.com • www.funcilitators.com

Comfort Food

Goal: Get to know new people, stretch your legs, and laugh.
Number of people: 8 to 24.
Time: 10 minutes.
Props: Cardstock (8 $\frac{1}{2}$" x 11"), colored markers.

Step-by-step:

1. In a classroom setting or during a regular workday when your co-workers are at their desks, take a break and have some fun.

2. Give each person a piece of card stock folded like a place card and provide the colored markers.

3. Ask each person to think of her favorite comfort food, defined as:
   a. What you like to eat when you've had a tough day
   b. What you eat when you deserve a treat, after an accomplishment
   c. What you eat in the middle of the night when no one's watching

4. Tell them what your own comfort food is, to get them laughing. (Mine's mayonnaise. With a spoon. Two scoops right in my mouth.)

5. Ask everyone to write their comfort food on one side of the cardstock tent, then go to a space in the room where you can all stand in a circle.

6. Go around the circle and let everyone name his comfort food, while holding up their tents.

7. Ask everyone to select a partner based on which comfort food would go well with theirs, and pair off.

8. Ask the pairs to take 3 minutes to brainstorm a party theme name, which would be appropriate for serving their two comfort foods (for instance, if ice cream and cookies were paired, the theme might be a "Vacation From Diets" party).

9. Invite them to come back into a circle and share their party themes.

10. Bonus: you may create some fun themes for your next recognition event.

Pair Up

Goal: Make team relationships more comfortable, and get the blood flowing.
Number of people: 8-24.
Time: 15-30 minutes, depending on group size.
Props: None.

Step-by-step:

1. During regular staff meetings or training sessions, open with a brief "Let's get to know each other even better" segment. This is especially useful when a new member has joined the group, or when the group is large and people don't have the opportunity to know all members well.

2. Use different criteria for assigning pairs at each meeting, so that each person finds herself getting to know a different person each time.

3. Ask the group to stand, then give them today's criterion for pairing.

4. Some ideas for pairings: Choose:

   a. Someone who is wearing the same color you are today
   b. The person you are least familiar with
   c. A long-term person with a short-term person
   d. Same shoe size
   e. Same birth month
   f. Same color vehicle
   g. Same number of children
   h. Born in same state or states closest geographically
   i. Same number of siblings
   j. Same favorite color
   k. Same favorite ice cream flavor
   l. _____

5. Most of these pairing criteria will necessitate people calling out words or phrases in order to find their partner. This adds to the energy and fun, and is a great way to get everyone's blood flowing to kick off your meeting.

6. After a few meetings, you might ask the group to brainstorm for additional new criteria for future meetings.

This idea created by: Janis Allen • janisallen@yahoo.com • www.janisallen.com

Dealing With Change

Goal: Demonstrate the discomfort of making changes and discuss healthy ways to handle it.

Number of people: 8-16.

Time: 20 minutes.

Props: None.

Step-by-step:

1. Just before taking a break at a meeting, give the group a specific time that you want them to return, such as 10:15. Tell them that it's important that everyone be present for the start of the first activity. Write this time on a board.

2. Instruct them to re-seat themselves when they return, alphabetically by name (you may select last name or first name, depending on how well they know each others' names).

3. You will all observe the few minutes of chaos and discomfort that ensues.

4. Ask them to move all their papers and belongings to the new seat.

5. Lead a discussion about dealing with change, asking:

   a. How did you feel before the break when I mentioned the change I wanted you to make?

   b. How did you feel after the break, once you began to make the change?

   c. What feelings and responses are natural when we encounter change?

   d. What are some healthy ways to deal with change?

   e. What changes in our organization can we relate this to?

6. Some conclusions may be that most of us dislike change and resist it, but that (1) allowing errors, (2) patience, and (3) looking for the benefits of the change will help us through in a healthy way.

You Made My Day

Goal: Energize a group and focus them on using positive recognition.
Number of People: 4 to 12.
Time: 10-20 minutes per meeting
Props: You Made My Day: Creating Co-Worker Recognition and Relationships, one copy per person.

Steps:

1. At your department meeting, give each person a copy of *You Made My Day.*
2. Ask everyone to select a two-page chapter to report on at your next meeting. Suggest they share one or two key ideas from the chapter, and tell a story from the chapter.
3. At the beginning of your next meeting, ask four people to report on their chapters. This gets everyone participating early, gets them energized, and keeps recognition in the forefront of their minds.
4. Everyone learns from all chapters reported without actually reading them.
5. Make a note of the chapters which have been reported.
6. Repeat at your next meeting, until most or all the chapters have been reported.

Created by: Janis Allen • janisallen@yahoo.com • www.janisallen.com

Jigsaw Puzzle

Goal: Boost the energy of a group during a meeting or sluggish afternoon.
Number of people: 8.
Time: 15 minutes.
Props: A jigsaw puzzle painted to replicate your organization's emblem or logo.

Step-by-step:

1. Make a large replica of your organization's emblem or logo, using tagboard (poster paper) or light wood.
2. Cut it into 20-30 pieces, jigsaw-puzzle style.
3. Mix the pieces and put them on a large table (or two tables together).
4. During a meeting break, invite attendees to assemble the puzzle.
5. Move quickly out of the way so you don't get stampeded!

This idea created by: Tina Pearson • Reported by: Jeanette Patton • Jeanette_Patton@adp.com
Automatic Data Processing, Folsom, CA

Appendix

To: Bernadette Casey

From: J. Roger Friedman

Subject: Headlines

Dear Bernadette:

I've been impressed with the headlines in the last few issues of Drug Store News.

They read well and gave a sense of urgency. The November 18th issue is an

example of what I am referring to – I liked the headlines on page 1 and on page 3.

The words "stunned" and "murky" are excellent choices of words.

Congratulations.

Roger

Sincerely,

J. Roger Friedman

Cc: Fred Filer, Marie Griffin, Bruce Matzner, Sandy Sutton

From You Made My Day: Creating Co-worker Recognition and Relationships, by Janis Allen and Michael McCarthy, 2000, L-F Books, NY, NY

To: Bernadette Casey

From: J. Roger Friedman

Subject: Headlines

Dear Bernadette:

I've been impressed with the headlines in the last few issues of Drug Store News. They read well and gave a sense of urgency. The November 18th issue is an example of what I am referring to – I liked the headlines on page 1 and on page 3. The words "stunned" and "murky" are excellent choices of words. Congratulations.

Sincerely,

Roger

J. Roger Friedman

Cc: Fred Filer, Marie Griffin, Bruce Matzner, Sandy Sutton

From You Made My Day: Creating Co-worker Recognition and Relationships, by Janis Allen and Michael McCarthy, 2000, L-F Books, NY, NY

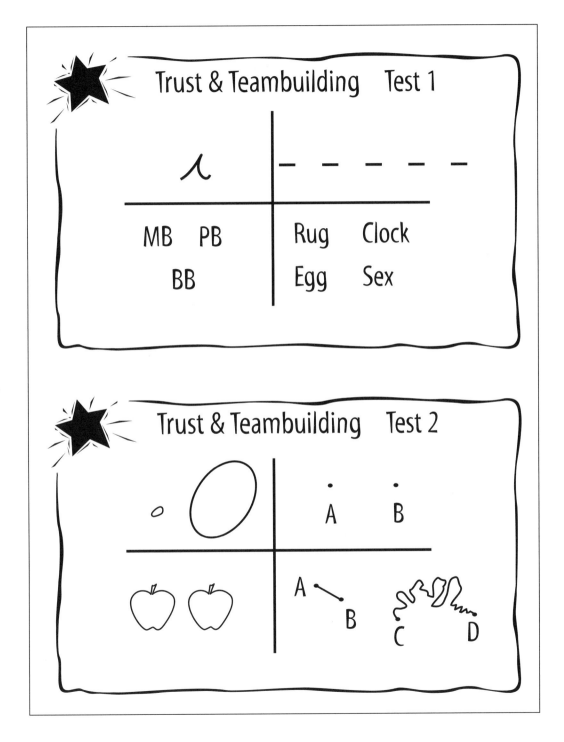

Maze Solution

Finish

	X				
X	X				
X		X	X	X	X
X	X	X			X
				X	X
				X	
		X	X	X	
		X			

Start

Used in The Maze, page 54.

117

Appendix

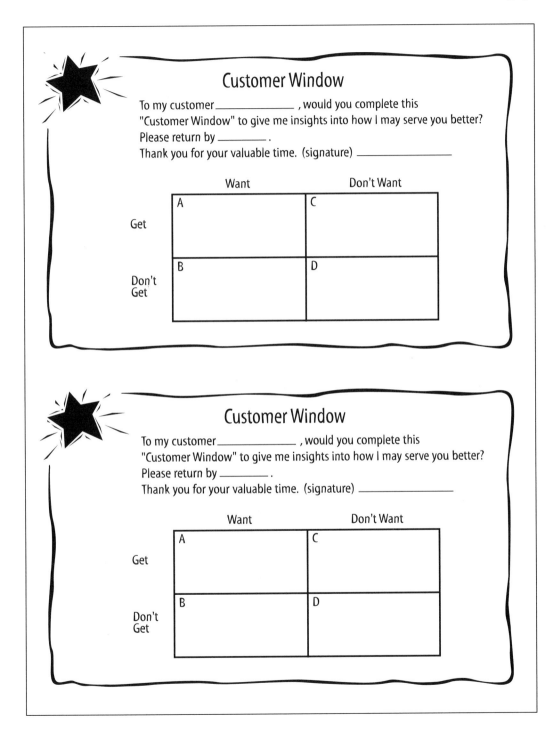

Customer Window

To my customer _____ , would you complete this
"Customer Window" to give me insights into how I may serve you better?
Please return by _____ .
Thank you for your valuable time. (signature) _____

	Want	Don't Want
Get	A	C
Don't Get	B	D

Customer Window

To my customer _____ , would you complete this
"Customer Window" to give me insights into how I may serve you better?
Please return by _____ .
Thank you for your valuable time. (signature) _____

	Want	Don't Want
Get	A	C
Don't Get	B	D

Used in Customer Window, page 71.

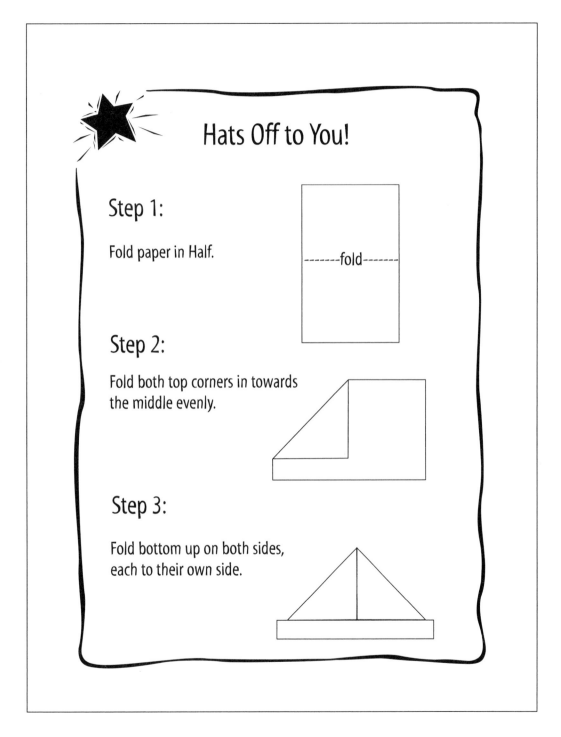

Hats Off to You!

Step 1:

Fold paper in Half.

-------fold-------

Step 2:

Fold both top corners in towards the middle evenly.

Step 3:

Fold bottom up on both sides, each to their own side.

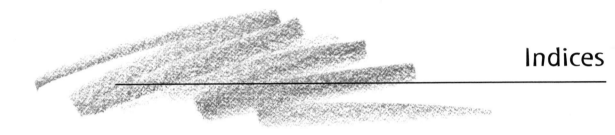

Indices

Indices

Index by Props

Index by Subject

You Make the Difference receipt cards 15
You Make the Difference reward seals 47
You Make the Difference Rich Rewards chocolates 39
You Make the Difference travel tumblers 20
You Make the Difference trifold paper 89
You Make the Difference trinket box 39
You Make the Difference umbrella 39
You Rock jumbo postcards 93

Anniversary 82, 83, 85, 87
Balloons 6, 12, 77, 84, 85, 88
Bingo 93
Birthday 86
Books 10, 41, 75
Brainstorm 7, 37, 108
Charades 71
Coach 55, 57, 72
Co-worker 6, 8, 9, 17, 18, 19, 20, 21, 23, 26, 28, 29, 32, 33, 39, 42, 43, 50, 56, 58, 61, 70, 76, 82, 85, 86, 89, 97, 103, 106
Customer Service 21, 27, 50, 65, 66, 67, 69, 70, 71, 72, 74, 75, 76, 86
e-mail 8, 10, 17, 65 ,68
Fish 13, 33, 54
Magic 20, 24
Patient Satisfaction 11
Photo 18, 20, 22, 51, 85, 89
Puzzle 107
Retirement 89, 90
Sole Mate 96
Stars 3, 4, 9, 18, 31, 42, 48, 66, 82, 88
Teacher 19, 54
Team 10, 20, 49, 55
Teamwork 10, 20, 49, 55
Training 29, 36, 104
Trivia 10
Trust 53, 73
Volunteers 12, 30, 31, 35, 41, 43, 54, 58, 69, 81, 83, 85, 95
Wall of Fame 20
Welcome 10, 20, 31, 81, 87, 88

Notes